COLUMBIA UNIVERSITY STUDIES IN ENGLISH
AND COMPARATIVE LITERATURE

POETIC IMAGERY

POETIC IMAGERY

ILLUSTRATED FROM ELIZABETHAN
LITERATURE

By
HENRY W. WELLS, Ph.D.

New York
RUSSELL & RUSSELL
1961

COPYRIGHT, 1924, 1951 BY COLUMBIA UNIVERSITY PRESS
PUBLISHED 1961 BY RUSSELL & RUSSELL, INC.
BY ARRANGEMENT WITH COLUMBIA UNIVERSITY PRESS
L. C. CATALOG CARD NO: 61–13091

821.3
W46

PRINTED IN THE UNITED STATES OF AMERICA

PREFACE

This book was written in 1918. The reader will at once perceive that I have left many important aspects of poetic imagery unnoticed. But since the ensuing study has seemed to contain a unity which would inevitably be lost by the introduction of new problems, I have presented my work in virtually its original form.

My warmest thanks are due to Professors George P. Krapp, Jefferson B. Fletcher, Ashley H. Thorndike and Charles Sears Baldwin, all of the Department of English and Comparative Literature in Columbia University, for aid which they have so generously afforded.

CONTENTS

POETIC IMAGERY

Illustrated From Elizabethan Literature

I

INTRODUCTION

The study of poetic imagery needs justification. Good
images are as a rule unpremeditated and enjoyed as instantaneously as a good jest. How a methodical study
might enable an author to employ better images or a reader
to enjoy imagery more is not obvious. It is possible that
a book on such a subject may at once be laid aside, with a
suspicion that the writer has failed to profit from M. Jour-
dain's lessons in rhetoric. More common sense is perhaps
to be found in this attitude than in the presentation of
metaphor and simile in our text books on rhetoric. Such
an attitude neglects, however, one of the most insistent
axioms of recent thought, the plasticity of habits. We can
by a study of imagery increase our appreciation of poetic
metaphor and become more effective in our own figures.
Such training is not at odds with spontaneity. A critical
study may shape to a considerable measure the spirit of our
imagination. A poem may be considered as a manuscript
sprinkled with phrases rapidly written in shorthand. These
phrases represent the metaphors, which are moments in
which the poet's imagination is working with the utmost
speed. Such rapidity of thought is difficult for all readers
to follow. When Shakespere writes ''I thought the King
had more affected the Duke of Albany than Cornwall,'' we

1

may easily approximate the poet's thought. But not so
when he writes:

> Men must endure
> Their going hence, even as their coming hither;
> *Ripeness* is all.
>
> *Lear,* V, 2, 9

The real difficulty is to follow the thought of the poet when
he writes in his great metaphorical language. One of the
chief purposes of this study is to interpret the leading characteristics of such abbreviated expression in poetry and
imaginative prose.

Metaphor has been treated in a methodical way from a
somewhat limited number of points of view. Rhetorical
distinctions have been made between the language-forms
of images. Hence come such terms as "metaphor" and
"simile" in the rhetorical sense. These distinctions may
on the whole be regarded as merely verbal, and hence as
blind alleys in thought. A different but still limited exercise is the consideration of the subject matter of the imaginative terms in a poet's metaphors. Lists have been made
of the number of figures in Shakespere taken from tailor-
ing, from animal life, or from aspects of the weather.
More important are studies in the relation of metaphor to
logic. Distinctions between metaphor and analogy, and an
understanding of the abuse called metaphorical logic, are
of general value. The psychologists have entered the larger
fields of symbolism and are laying there the foundations of
a new science. But in spite of a profusion of casual criticism, few methodical studies of poetic imagery have been
made from the standpoint of its technique or its imaginative value. Scholarship has here advanced little beyond
the work of the classical rhetoricians. The present study
attempts in a methodical manner to trace the character and
degree of imaginative activity in poetic metaphor. Although there may be no assurance that the inquiry so begun

will develop further, there seems no reason to hesitate in planting the seed.

An additional attraction is found in the turning up of old ground in new furrows. As the line of our inquiry progresses we shall at least be brought in contact at new angles with the philosophy, temperament and manners of poets in a celebrated literary age. Radically different practices in metaphor among contemporary writers give still an additional interest to the theme. Few periods in literary history show a greater variety in this respect than our own. While many authors are consciously cultivating an original figurative style, others studiously avoid all but the faintest traces of metaphor. Symbolists who have called each other decadent, robust, impressionistic and oriental have striven somewhat unsympathetically with one another and with the advocates of classical or scientific severity. Is there not room for a broad, theoretical and methodical treatment of the subject? Various causes, then, provoke such a treatment. Poetic imagery is a plastic habit. The treatment is relatively new. New light should incidentally be thrown on adjacent fields. Finally there seems special occasion from a confusion in contemporary practice.

The study faces many difficulties. It is difficult to estimate the subject in its bearings and to pursue it with caution and restraint. The popular estimate of its significance has suffered from an early association of symbolism with rhetoric, not, as one might wish, with religion, philosophy, idealism and humor. Poetic imagery has been discussed as though it were a distinctly literary matter, like a point in dramatic technique, and not an element in the very air we breathe. For example, much of the division between Catholics and Protestants from the sixteenth to the present century has been caused by divergent attitudes toward imagery. In this Introduction I shall attempt to describe the bearing and significance of the subject, to define its terms and to describe what appears to be a secure line for critical inquiry. I shall first indicate how persistent metaphor is, how it is a natural language of the emotions and how valuable it is in symbolizing our institutions and ideals.

Although aspersions are sometimes cast on metaphorical thought, as though it were tainted by a contact with metaphorical logic, it must be accepted as an undiminishing activity. English poetry begins with a highly wrought, impetuous and imaginative style, but not an exceptionally figurative style. Anglo-Saxon verse probably appears today more figurative than it really is, for many of the compounds which are fresh and figurative to us were no doubt already somewhat faded by constant use. Through the entire range of English literature however few writers are more vigorous in the making of symbols than Browning, George Eliot, Meredith and Hardy. Though an historical study would no doubt show that the character of metaphor changes, there is no evidence that metaphor in western thought diminishes in degree. If primitive and exuberantly undisciplined forms decline in use, we may assume that more sophisticated ones take their place.

If a scientific training is unfavorable to some types of imagery, it is distinctly favorable to others. The contrast between scientific thought and metaphorical thought is not far to seek. Analogy, for example, is of considerable value in scientific thinking. An analogy between two ideas is an assumption of similarity expressible as a general law. Analogy is the next step from metaphor in the direction of scientific thought. In fact it is not always possible to distinguish between metaphor and analogy. In science a creative mind which has the imagination to profit by analogies will presumably in moments of relaxation from rigorous thinking have some capacity for metaphor. Shakespere sums up a view of the moral life in the metaphorical phrase "ripeness is all." Newton by the analogy of a falling apple conceives an idea of the universe governed by gravitation, and by a systematic investigation he later transforms an analogy into a scientific theory. The minds of the poet and the scientist are here seen to approximate each other. It is in fact almost as improbable that one who is notable for literal-mindedness should be a creative scientist as that he should be a creative artist. Letter writing and the less formal modes of expression often show in the scientific genius a marked predilection for metaphor. Bacon, Huxley and Tyndall in their writings which are not technical show a poetic imagery not far removed from that of the more figurative of the poets. Far from damaging a capacity for metaphor, a scientific training may discipline the mind in respect to imagery for even greater effectiveness. When the physicist unbends his fancy the universe shakes with laughter through his imagery. A review of some typical metaphors by men of science may be suggestive. There is for example a story that when a stranger to the world of science asked Franklin the mocking question, "But what is this experiment good for?" the philosopher retorted: "But what is a new born child good for?" In making the cultural implications of evolution felt by the general public Huxley became profuse in metaphor. Something of his exuberance may be seen in the following sentence:

Extinguished theologians lie about the cradle of every science as the strangled snakes beside that of Hercules.

Darwiniana, p. 52

In a popular manual the ideals of scientific thought are expressed in a figurative manner:

The retirement of the student from hourly pressure of the world is as necessary as setting apart the milk pan to let the cream rise. The mistake arises when we begin to think of this isolation as the sole essential and overlook that all the cream we get comes from the cow.

Geddes and Thomson, *Evolution,* p. 217

The metaphors of Bacon were the trumpet calls that summoned modern science to arms. Not only have the ideals of science been enforced by the eloquence of metaphor, but philosophers have denounced the intrusiveness of imagery into rigorous thinking by the most effective metaphors of their own.

On the contrary metaphors and senseless and ambiguous words are like *ignis fatui,* and reasoning upon them is wandering amongst innumerable absurdities.

Hobbes, *Leviathan,* 1, 5

Nothing is more dangerous to reason than the flights of the imagination, and nothing has been the occasion of more mistakes among the philosophers. Men of bright fancies may in this respect be compared to those angels whom the Scriptures represent as covering their eyes with their wings.

Hume, *Treatise of Human Nature,* Book I, IV, 7

One of the least figurative authors may be associated with the cause of imagery. To John Stuart Mill we owe the familiar quotation, itself a paraphrase from Bacon, which likens marriage to a giving of hostages to Mrs. Grundy. Extreme literal-mindedness seems very generally to be viewed as a defect. Hayraddin, a character in Scott's *Quentin Durward,* is of exceptional interest as an illustration of this generally unsympathetic, matter-of-fact type. The most literal-minded story writer in his vigorous passages will often fall into some form of metaphor. Thus Defoe in a famous passage of Robinson Crusoe breaks into an image suggesting a passage in one of the most figurative of all Shakespere's plays.

As I walked about either in my hunting or for viewing the country, the anguish of my soul at my condition would break out upon me on a sudden and my very heart die within me to think of the woods, the mountains, the deserts I was in, and how I was a prisoner, locked up with the eternal bars and bolts of the ocean, in an unhabited wilderness, without redemption.

I, 8

A similar imagination animates these lines:

> and it is great
> To do that thing that ends all other deeds,
> Which shackles accidents, and bolts up change.
> *Ant. and Cleo.* V, 2, 3

Swift possessed a most ardent metaphorical mind. Though in Gulliver's Travels he affected a simple, straightforward style, half the book is based on the fundamentally metaphorical idea that the diminutive is mean and the gigantic gross. In short, scientists such as Huxley and Tyndall, philosophers such as Hume and Mill, a thoroughgoing literally minded genius like Defoe, or a genius who assumes the matter-of-fact style as does Swift, all exhibit some power in imagery.

What are the circumstances which arouse poetic imagery? We have observed it in the expression of ideals. The more resonant imagination appears under some pressure of emotion, and often with some relaxation of rigorous thinking. Wine it may be observed is a great breeder of imagery. The idea of intoxication itself is sufficient to evoke a flood of metaphors. Picturesque drinking terms are innumerable. Harrison for example gives us the Elizabethan terms "mad dog," "angel's food," "dragon's milk," etc. Contemporary epithets are almost as reckless and fantastical. Whatever may be the objects of our affection, we address them metaphorically. The Elizabethans lavished images upon their mistresses. There is a great number of figures for the dollar. Metaphor also rises from fear or taboo. Many euphemistic terms soften the bitterness of the word death. As the language of the emotions

metaphor is the language of poetry. The restriction of
this study to the images of poetry or of poetic prose rests
on this assumption. Many men of genius have cast their
thought in a perplexing shroud of metaphor, as did Swift
and Carlyle. Swift at least guarded against objections,
wittily describing the relation between genius and a profusion of imagery. Wisdom, he writes, "is a hen whose
cackling we must value and consider because it is attended
with an egg." Should anyone find some instances of vain
metaphorical cackling in a work of genius, he will probably
find no end of it well paid for if accompanied by such brilliant images of apprehension as many in the *Tale of a Tub*.
Satire, to cite one of them, Swift calls "a butt bandied to
and fro, and every man carries a racket about with him to
strike it from himself among the rest of the company."
One thinks of all that Ruskin lost and gained through his
figurative exuberance. Surely there is some profit in self-
knowledge on such a subject.

The social significance of imagery is perhaps best revealed, however, from the historical point of view. Many
ideas of the medieval church are, it appears, no more remote from us to-day than the metaphorical language in
which these ideas were expressed. Two tendencies in the
medieval practice nevertheless may be distinguished.
While scholasticism had at times a truly literal-minded devotion to allegory, the ritual of the church manifested a
superb religious symbolism. Although there is a continual
demand for an effective metaphorical expression of ideals,
there was only a passing zest for the idea that the world is
a puzzle in metaphor. Much of the scholastic allegorizing
is as dead as anything well can be. So far however as the
medieval mind was able to humanize by metaphor and personification, by ritual and by ceremony, what were actually
its guiding passions, it possessed an enviable power. Mag-
nificently for example is the doctrine of the Trinity figured

in the three towers of Lincoln Cathedral. We may be sure that Hugh of Lincoln and those who laid stone upon stone believed in the doctrine of Holy Church. Or take the culminating image in *Piers Plowman:* Christ, or the body of true Christians, plowing with the four gospels the field which is the world. A faith is not easily relinquished which is made visible and brought home by such imagery as this.

Though imagery to-day may perform a more varied work, one may question if any considerable number of our modern ideals are as impressively symbolized as those which motivated medieval life. Yet much of the dignity of an institution and the loyalty which it commands rests on the success with which its ideals are symbolized.

Not only does a study of imagery as the effective expression of commanding social ideas naturally become in part historical, but national distinctions are suggested. In England since the age of Ben Jonson the use of symbolism in public ceremony is generally unsatisfying. On the other hand such imagery seems still to have retained something of its medieval vigor in the Latin countries. Though relatively few new types or ideas are found in their ceremonies and although personifications are often lacking in a strong metaphorical element, a considerable imaginative power remains. While English poetry is perhaps richer in metaphor than the poetry of the Romance languages, metaphorical ceremony seems to flourish with greater distinction among the Latin races. The English people may be said to excel in the transient image of poetry, and the Romance peoples in establishing conventional metaphors for popular abstractions in the pictorial arts.

During a visit of the Prince of Wales to New York in 1919 an American battleship at anchor near the flagship of the Prince complimented him during the night with an electrical display of his profile hung between the masts.

The personality of this allusion is the antithesis of what
might be expected from the Gallic or the medieval mind.
To the medieval mind the temporal ruler signified the
power of God incarnate in the state. Shakespere's King
Harry on the evening before Agincourt recalled the emblems of his royalty:

> the balm, the sceptre and the ball,
> The sword, the mace, the crown imperial,
> The intertissued robe of gold and pearl,
> The farced title running 'fore the king.
>
> *Hen. V,* IV, 1, 277

These symbols have gone with the conception of divine
right. But where it may be asked are the new symbols
of democratic right? It should be added that these at-
tributes of the king were at times thought of as objects of
a supernatural nature in themselves, and consequently
were something more than the mere emblems of royalty.
Men blind to political facts laid down their lives for a
metaphor. Judges, relying on the awe which surrounded
the insignia of justice, shamefully perverted justice. Sick
men drank liquid gold from pure metaphorical logic. That
metaphor is not rigorous thinking does not however pre-
clude its being the decoration and the consecration of wisdom more solidly attained. With quaint and beautiful
imagery Dekker has said of honesty that "she goes upon
lame feet unless there be music in her." So the best of
men and of institutions without some gift of metaphorical
expression go limping through their existence.

The preceding paragraphs have sketched the inevitable-
ness, the general character and the functions of metaphorical thought from its more favorable aspects. The aim has
been to illustrate what sort of excellencies the reader may
find or desire to find in the figures classified and cited in
the ensuing chapters. Although the main study is purely
descriptive, images are chosen to invite the evaluative criti-

cism of the reader. Only in the Introduction are the out-
lines of evaluative criticism suggested, and these drawn
only in the broadest lines. It remains however to illustrate
some typical accusations against metaphor, which it may
be supposed will be paralleled by the reader's own objections to figures cited in later sections. Adverse criticism
falls broadly under three heads. Metaphor is said to induce faults in reasoning and faults in taste, and to contribute to a moral diffusion. The logician, the critic and the
moralist find offences against judgment, taste and personality. They may speak for themselves. In the capacity of
a logician George Eliot writes in *The Mill on the Floss*.
Mr. Tulliver grapples somewhat feebly with his wife's
views on figurative thought.

" Well, well, we won't send him out o' reach o' the carrier's
cart, if other things fit in," said Mr. Tulliver. " But you
mustn't put a spoke i' the wheel about the washin', if we can't
get a school near enough. That's the fault I have to find wi'
you, Bessy; if you see a stick i' the road you're allys thinkin'
you can't step over it. You'd want me not to hire a good
wagoner, 'cause he'd got a mole on his face."

" Dear heart," said Mrs. Tulliver in mild surprise, " when did
I iver make objections to a man because he'd got a mole on his
face? I'm sure I'm rether fond o' moles, for my brother, as
is dead an' gone, had a mole on his brow. But I can't remember you iver offering to hire a wagoner with a mole, Mr. Tulliver. There was John Gibbs hadn't a mole on his face no
more nor you have, an' I was all for having you hire him; an'
so you did hire him, an' if he hadn't died o' th' inflammation
as we paid Dr. Turnball for attending him, he'd very like ha'
been driving the wagon now. . . .

" No, no, Bessy; I didn't mean justly the mole; I meant it to
stand for summat else. But niver mind; it's puzzling work
talking is."

This may be taken as a fair instance of the disastrous
consequences of metaphorical language to good reasoning

in popular talk. But if George Eliot found imagery destructive to the interests of the Tullivers, she found it equally destructive to the accepted theories of a gentleman's education. In a later chapter of the same book she illustrates the metaphorical fallacy not in talk but in argument. Mrs. Tulliver and the Rev. Mr. Stirlling are on common ground.

It was his favorite metaphor that the classics and geometry constituted that culture of the mind which prepared it for the reception of any subsequent crop. I say nothing against Mr. Stirlling's theory. I only know that it turned out as uncomfortably for Tom Tulliver as if he had been plied with cheese in order to remedy a gastric weakness which prevented him from digesting it.

It is astonishing what a different result one gets by changing the metaphor. Once call the brain an intellectual stomach, and one's ingenious conception of the classics and geometry as ploughs and harrows seems to settle nothing. But then it is open to someone else to follow great authorities, and call the mind a sheet of white paper or a mirror, in which case one's knowledge of the digestive process becomes quite irrelevant. It was doubtless an ingenious idea to call the camel the ship of the desert, but it would hardly lead one far in training that useful beast. O Aristotle, if you had had the advantage of being " the freshest modern " instead of the greatest ancient, would you not have mingled your praise of metaphorical speech as a sign of high intelligence with a lamentation that intelligence so rarely shows itself in speech without metaphor—that we can so seldom declare what a thing is, except by saying it is something else.

II, 1

Both Mrs. Tulliver and, one would judge, the Rev. Mr. Stirlling lost a clear view of an issue by taking the left hand turn at the metaphor. There is however a contrast. Mrs. Tulliver was under no illusion. She had merely changed the subject. She had failed to keep on the more immediate topic of her son's schooling. Mr. Stirlling on the other hand believed himself to be commenting on education, when in fact the chief merit of his discussion must have remained in its fragments of pastoral imagery. Mrs. Tulliver did not spoil either of her two subjects so long as she was faithful to it. Mr. Stirlling confusing his two ideas damaged each. Once Mr. Stirlling conceived his image from husbandry, he was fortified against a new view of his subject. To such an image one may attach an unanswerableness which no line of literal thought may possess. From these illustrations, then, two types of metaphor may be derived in relation to their logical value. Mrs. Tulliver illustrates the Digressive image, Mr. Stirlling the Insistent.

Hobbes, as we have seen, was opposed to the metaphorical exuberance of Elizabethan thinkers, though the title of his own masterpiece is sufficiently fanciful. After observing the injury sustained by truth from the digressive symbol, he discusses what may be called the prejudicial image. He says: "In orations of praise and in invectives the fancy is predominant, because the design is not truth, but to honor or dishonor, which is done by noble or vile comparisons." Metaphor is the first tool seized by the eulogist or the detractor. By the black art of metaphor damaging evidence is concealed, an outlook is confined, or the mind extravagantly prejudiced to praise or blame. Poe says in a droll phrase in his *Marginalia:* "The nose of a mob is its imagination; by this at any time it can be quietly led."

Such are some of the observations of men of letters on the logic of imagery. It may further be observed how naturally a fanciful and beautiful image may satisfy the mind and discourage a rude breaking of the image in the interests of literal investigation. The seductive powers of figurative explanations, like those of mythology or beast legend, are often so true to the human heart that the public cares not whether they are true to nature. This is notably the case with the medieval mind, and with the youthful period of the English Renaissance. Science cannot compete without a struggle against reasoning in such images as these on dreams by Thomas Nash.

Divers have written diversely of their causes, but the best reason among them all that I could ever pick out was this: that as an arrow which is shot out of a bow is sent forth many times with such force that it flyeth far beyond the mark whereat it was aimed, so our thoughts . . . fly beyond the mark of the day into the confines of the night. To nothing more aptly can I compare the working of our brains after we have . . . gone to bed, than to the glimmering and dazzling of a man's eyes when he comes newly out of the bright sun into the dark shadow.

I, 355

The laboring men's hands glow and blister after their day's work; and the glowing and blistering of our brains after our day laboring cogitations are dreams.

III, 197

This "best reason" of Nash is avowedly little more than a poetic fancy. Of slightly greater pretension is the nimble and affected metaphorical logic of Lyly. But early writers were much more earnest in this kind. Sir Thomas Elyot holds, for example, that Nature is our kindly teacher. If her face is read aright the meaning is always symbolical. Nature does not share the contamination of flesh, as in Puritan thought, nor do her controlling laws, as in scientific thought, appear significant to the reflecting man. Nature is a design of bright and alluring images wrought by God to win man to Him. This conception appears in the following figurative defence of the autocratic state.

One sun ruleth over the day and one moon over the night; and to descend down to the earth, in a little beast, which of all others is most to be marvelled at, I mean the bee, is left to man

by Nature, as it seemeth, a perpetual figure of a just governance
or rule.

The Governour, I, 2

Obvious as survivals of a purely medieval form of metaphorical reasoning are elaborate moralizings of the dance
in the same book.

The fashion of reenforcing an argument with ornate and
conventional images affected even the economic pamphlets
of Defoe. He writes on banking in a manner now discredited: "Allowing those many banks could without
clashing maintain a constant correspondence with one another in passing each other's bills as current from one another, I know not it might be better performed by one, for
as harmony makes music in sound, so it produces success
in business."

Turning from accusations against metaphor as hostile to
sound reasoning, one may consider what critics have
thought abuses of good taste. Matthew Arnold describes
taste as an ancient, continental mode of thought, characteristic of the central peoples in the history of European culture. Bad taste fails to rise to cosmopolitan standards, and
lacks the self-control required for the utmost effectiveness.
One section of Arnold's essay, *The Literary Influence of
Academies,* is essentially an arraignment of exuberant
metaphorical expression. Although he reconciles the fault
to genius, he criticizes it none the less severely. Citing a
passage practically without imagery from Bossuet as an
illustration of good taste, he quotes one passage from
Jeremy Taylor and four from Burke to illustrate "Asiatic" prose. The English passages are excessively figurative.

An observation made by G. M. Trevelyan in the Introduction to his *Poetry and Philosophy of George Meredith*
contains criticism of a highly metaphorical author by one
of his foremost critics. Mr. Trevelyan says: "Whenever

he fails it is not through want but through excess of imagination; his metaphors sometimes strive, one on the back of
another, like fierce animals in a pit.'' The images attributed here to Meredith resemble those of Burke, and fall
under Arnold's category of language offensive to good
taste.

The third offence ascribed to imagery though more serious is less readily examined. Not only may it cloud judgment and distort taste, but aid evasion and in excess dis-
turb personal stability. Exuberant imagery makes for diffusion. The mind becomes a mirror for the first suggestions from the immediate physical world. Literature affords innumerable illustrations of impersonality and imaginative profusion. These characteristics are among the
tragic faults of Shakespere's Richard II, the victim of every
figurative suggestion. An exceptional fluency in metaphor
appears at times in Boswell's own talk, and his personality
is wax. The earlier Romances of Greene are a dissipation
in metaphor, as the author himself was a pipe for Fortune's
finger. One may catch a snatch of the same quality in a
phrase from Dekker's *Wonderful Year*. The grave is ''the
wild Irish country of worms.'' A subdued imagination
would not toy on the grave with metaphor; but the vinous
spirit of Elizabethan fancy gained a somewhat questionable
victory over the ills of life. This recklessness is not pleas-
ing to all. The overcharged atmosphere in which such imagery breeds is depicted by Nash. ''If in the dead of night
there be any knocking or disturbance near us, we straight
dream of wars or of thunder. If a dog howl we suppose
we are transported into hell, where we hear the complaint
of damned ghosts'' (I, 356). Dream symbolism and path-
ological symbolism however do not come under the general
scope of this discussion. An instance of the latter may be
taken from Lear's wild words of self pity,

> the little dogs and all,
> Tray, Blanch and Sweetheart, see, they bark at me.

III, 6, 65

We have now seen something of the alleged abuse of logic, taste and personality by metaphor. After a review of the strength and beauty of metaphorical thought on the one hand, and a survey of its intimate association with weakness and error on the other, and with an understanding of the plasticity of the habit, the significance of the study of imagery becomes somewhat clearer.

A particular body of literary material must be selected for observation. This leads to the question what restrictions are advisable. Although the term poetic imagery is of course used in a much broader sense than imagery in verse, it is clear that verse will in fact comprise the larger and more fruitful part of our material. Poetry is a tropical zone of metaphor. There figures are thickest and most variegated. Our attention will, then, be given largely to poetry, but by no means confined to it. To restrict the study to a single author would be unwise. Few authors supply material for a comprehensive investigation. The most favorable ground is a literary age. In the ideal age for this investigation the types of metaphor should be abundant, they should reflect antecedent periods and be reflected in subsequent ones, they should be consciously used, and frequently criticized during the years that separate that age from our own. English literature during the lifetime of Shakespere best fulfills these requirements.

The age of Shakespere is of peculiar interest to the student of poetic metaphor. Its use of metaphorical ceremony, its contact with usages abroad, its inheritance from medieval imagery, its influence upon the practice of later English poetry, the historical and contemporary criticism which it received, its extraordinary scope and its culmination in the imagery of Shakespere, all give it exceptional value. Beauty, passion, philosophy, and humor find in it rare figurative expression. In no period, on the contrary, have we more extreme conceits or more extravagant fustian.

The Elizabethans effectively used metaphorical emblems and embodied abstractions in their public ceremony. In their age alone English usages in this regard rivalled those in Italy and France. The decline of the symbolic fête in England begins with the passing of Elizabethan pageantry from the streets and the masque from the stage. From Italian, French and Spanish the Elizabethans notoriously borrowed metaphors ranging from the trivial conceits of Serafino to figurative conventions in the rituals of ancient poetry. Many passages in their poems, such as the description of the House of Charity in *The Fairie Queene,* show that animation had not passed from medieval imagery, nor had the old technique been lost. Elizabethan imagery has had a notable effect on the history of English poetry. One century illustrates its deterioration, another a revolt from it, and a third shows more often a sedulous imitation of its form than a grasp of its spirit. It has received abundant criticism. Swinburne for example has written luminously on the imagery of George Chapman. He observes that Chapman smothers himself in metaphor, while Browning is said to be accelerated and impelled by the symbol-making power. As spokesman for the classical age Johnson indirectly attacked the earlier imagery as merely ingenious or barbaric. A citation from the *Life of Addison* illustrates his view of a figure that suggests an Elizabethan type.

> Fir'd with that name
> I bridle in my struggling Muse with pain
> That longs to launch into a nobler strain.

To bridle a goddess is no very delicate idea; but why must she be bridled? because she longs to launch; and whither will she launch? into a nobler strain. She is in the first line a horse, in the second a boat, and the care of the poet is to keep his horse or his boat from singing.

The Elizabethans in their own criticism show themselves

aware of a conflict of ideals in imagery.   No discussion of
their general criticism of metaphor enters into the present
scheme.   Some recognition however may be made of Elizabethans commenting upon themselves.   Ben Jonson is the
leading spokesman for imaginative restraint.   In his *Dis-
coveries* he commends the following viewpoint.   ''His subtlety did not show itself; his judgment thought that a vice;
for the ambush hurts more than is hid.   He never forced
his language, nor went out of the highway of speaking but
for some great necessity or apparent profit; for he denied
figures to be invented for ornament, but for aid; and still
thought it an extreme madness to bend or wrest that which
ought to be right.''   Of a different opinion were Gascoigne,
the soldier poet, and the young Spenser.   Gascoigne writes
in his essay on poetry: ''If I should declare my pretensions
in love . . . I would use the covertest means that I could
to avoid the uncomely customs of common writers.''   This
thought lies at the bottom of much of the imagery in the
lyric poetry of the period.   Much the same opinion is expressed in Spenser's First Letter to Harvey.   After some
fantastic trifling over love, an earthquake and a game of
cards, the poet continues:

Extra Jocum, I did like your dramas passing well; and the
rather because they savour of that singular extraordinary vein
of invention, which I ever fancied most and in a manner admired only in Lucian, Petrarch, Aretino, Pasquill and all
Italians (for the Romans to speak of are but very ciphers in
this kind) whose chiefest endeavor and drift was to have nothing vulgar, but in some respect or other, and especially in
lively hyperbolical amplifications, rare, quaint and odd in every
point, and as a man would say a degree or two at least above
the reach and compass of a common scholar's capacity.

. The Elizabethan age is a windfall of the imagination.
Few types of metaphor remain undiscovered in the zest for
imaginative exercise.   The phenomena of life received

metaphorical explanations, as we have seen dreams explained by the fancy of Thomas Nash. Sir Walter Raleigh's servant is said to have seen his master wreathed in smoke, and thinking that his head had caught fire from too rigorous thinking drenched him forthwith in a bucket of water. With suggestion going at so fantastic a pace little in imagery from the trivial to the sublime, in poetry, religion or philosophy, escaped the English public of the later sixteenth century. Englishmen became keenly aware of the objective elements in vocabulary. No restrictions of poetic decorum kept them from drawing their loftiest metaphors from sticks and straw. Their imagery has been much commented upon casually, and studied from a few rather limited points of view. The first purpose of this study is to disclose some of the bases of poetic imagery by a review of Elizabethan metaphor. Its secondary purpose is to disclose some of the chief tendencies in the imagery of English poetry during the lifetime of Shakespere. The eminence of Elizabethan literature commands a spacious view backward to the medieval and forward to the modern period.

What in the body of literature selected for attention is to be regarded as poetic metaphor? What is the test for the ore to be drawn from our literary mine? We may first determine what is metaphor, and then what is poetic metaphor.

Since poetry is art, and the associative symbol may be called symbolism without art, it may be omitted from a study of poetic imagery. The same may be said of unconscious symbolism. This is the lively sequence of suggestions that shifts unconsciously the train of our thought. In Poe's *Murders of the Rue Morgue* a detective reveals the sequence of thought through which his friend silently passes under the suggestion of objects seen in the street as they walk. Psychologists have studied both these types of symbolism. There is too much of peculiar interest in Elizabethan literature to pause over these familiar categories. Poetic imagery is metaphorical, and to metaphor our interest will be restricted.

No strict definition of metaphor is I believe possible. By this I mean that no two people can so define the term that in any considerable body of poetry they will agree as to what does or does not constitute the metaphorical thoughts. A working test is however quite practicable. Metaphor is the recognition of a suggestion of one concept by another dissimilar in kind but alike in some strong ungeneric characteristic. If fancy is called "dream footed as the shadow of a cloud," fancy and the cloud are recognized as generically distinct, but alike in ineffectual fleetness. This is metaphor. The idea can be illustrated by the use of geometric circles which are neither congruent nor removed, but at some points intersect. By means of these circles the exclusion of non-metaphorical terms as too nearly congruent or too far removed may be graphically expressed.

Two types of symbolism that give congruent circles are analogy and exemplification. In each the terms are alike in kind. An instance of what is presumably to be taken for analogy appears in these lines from *Troilus and Cressida*.

> How may I avoid,
> Although my will distaste what it elected,
> The wife I chose? There can be no evasion
> To blench from this and to stand firm by honor.
> We turn not back the silks upon the merchant
> When we have soil'd them.

II, 2, 65

If the obligations to wife and merchant represent a common principle of justice the passage is not metaphorical. There is no sufficient distinction in kind. If however one holds that no logical relation is intended, the figure is a metaphor. Analogy is a logical, exemplification a literary, figure. Johnson has well illustrated the identity of the circles in exemplification. After noting that the figure of the angel in Addison's Campaign has been called one of the noblest thoughts that ever entered into the mind of man and is "therefore worthy of attentive consideration," the critic continues:

A poetical simile is the discovery of likeness between two actions in their general nature dissimilar, or of causes terminating by different operations in the same resemblance of effect. But the mention of another like consequence from a like cause, or of a like performance by a like agency, is not a simile but an exemplification. It is not a simile to say that the Thames waters fields as the Po waters fields. . . . When Horace says of Pindar that he pours his violence and rapidity of verse as a river swollen with rain rushes from the mountain; or of himself, that his genius wanders in quest of poetical decorations as the bee wanders to collect honey; he in either case produces a simile; the mind is impressed with the resemblance of things generally unlike, as unlike as intellect and body. Marlborough is so like the angel in the poem that the action of both is almost the same, and performed by both in the same manner. Marlborough "teaches the battle to rage"; the angel directs the storm; Marlborough is "unmoved in peaceful thought"; the angel is "calm and serene"; Marlborough stands "unmoved amidst the shock of hosts"; the angel rides "calm in the whirlwind." The lines on Marlborough are just and noble; but the simile gives almost the same images a second time.

But perhaps this thought, though hardly a simile, was remote from vulgar conceptions, and required great labor of research or dexterity of application. Of this, Dr. Madden . . . once gave me his opinion. "If I had set," said he, "ten school boys to write on the battle of Blenheim, and eight had brought me the angel, I should not have been surprised."

In the first of these paragraphs Johnson shows his vigorous

common sense. In the second both he and Dr. Madden prove themselves superior to the common taste of their day. They observe that exemplification has no imaginative power comparable to metaphor. Those who could mistake the image of the angel for a simile, or in the present terminology a metaphor, must have been slow in discriminating the types of symbolic imagination.

Among the images superficially and distantly related to metaphor are the pun and arbitrary sign symbolism. The latter is illustrated in the algebraical symbols. It is even further removed from metaphor than the associative symbol, for the sign symbol is arbitrary to all and has a precise significance, while the associative symbol is inevitable to at least a single person and may be highly stimulating to the imagination. The pun and the sign symbol may be figured as tangent circles.

The Comparison suggests three circular sheets of glass, one a colored transparency held before the other two and surrounding them. Again the likeness is superficial and precise. Take for example the thought that the sky is as grey as lead. The only similarity is one of color. This is not poetic metaphor. Neither is it poetic imagery to compare a cloud to a whale. The only similarity is one of shape. In every poetic metaphor there must be a subjective element. If a sportsman likens a drooping flag to the corpse of a brilliant bird, his image exceeds a comparison of physical objects. There is a suggestion of sadness or even of death in the listless flag hanging about its pole. To the mind of the sportsman naturally comes the idea of the bright body of a dead bird. This is a poetic metaphor. The image of the cloud and whale is metaphor but not poetic metaphor. The thought of a common greyness in lead and sea shows a sharper division of the idea into three parts instead of two, and consequently is a departure from symbolism itself. The poetic image may be called sympathetic or prejudicial.

Some difficulty arises in distinguishing metaphor and synecdoche. In synecdoche there are not two circles but one with a segment in emphasis. The difficulty is, figuratively, to determine whether the second term is an independent circle or a segment of the first.

Quite as perplexing as the distinction between metaphor and unmetaphorical symbolism, or between the poetic and the unsympathetic metaphor, is the distinction between imagery and literal statement in the matter of vocabulary. The word "dissection" for example might in this regard be ambiguous. Are two terms contained in this word or only one? Words which are possibly but not probably metaphorical, and especially words which have had figurative meanings which have since been dropped, may be called faded images. Most of our derivative Latin compounds illustrate the faded figure.

If much that is sometimes considered metaphor may well be excluded from our present consideration, much that is not thought of as imagery by the rhetoricians may be included. Their categories are based on formal distinctions of language. When content and not form is the test, that which might otherwise be taken for literal thought becomes figurative. To describe this large class it is necessary to distinguish two types into which all metaphor may be divided. These are the Direct and the Inverse. Direct images are often unobserved by rhetorical criticism.

Every metaphorical relation is composed of a major and a minor term, distinguished by the greater importance attached to the former. If someone should admire a drooping flag and think it like a bird's body, we may suppose him more attached to the flag than to the bird. If on the other hand a torn flag should suggest a nation divided against itself, we may suppose that the passing sight of a damaged flag leads to the more important thought of national dissension. In the first case, something of primary

importance already in the eye and mind, a flag, receives
supplementary emphasis and interpretation from a secondary idea, the bird. This is Inverse Metaphor. In the
second case something of secondary importance, the flag,
gives renewed vigor to an idea of primary importance, the
nation. This is Direct Metaphor. It occurs when the term
which is the immediate cause of the suggestion is thought
of as the less important. Inverse Metaphor occurs when
the term which is the immediate cause of the suggestion is
thought of as the more important. Inverse Metaphor is
more frequently met with in life than in literature, because in literature we are as a rule more conscious of people
than of the physical scenes which they inhabit. In our
daily experience images are forced upon us by nature.
More especially in dramatic literature, however, the mind
draws consciously upon its memory of natural objects to
illustrate sensations and ideas. In this regard the modern
stage is closer to life than the Elizabethan. In the dramas
of Oscar Wilde, Maeterlinck, D'Annunzio and Hugo von
Hofmannsthal characters are far more susceptible to suggestion from the physical scene than are those on the Elizabethan stage. Direct Metaphor, however, appears more
frequently there than on the stage of Molière. An illustration of the physical scene affording a metaphorical idea
may be taken from *Cymbeline*. Belarius and his two sons
are coming at sunrise from their cave:

> A goodly day not to keep house, with such
> Whose roof's as low as ours! Stoop, boys; this gate
> Instructs you how to adore the heaven's and bows you
> To the morning's holy office. The gates of monarchs
> Are arched so high that giants may jet through
> And keep their impious turbans on, without
> Good morrow to the sun.

III, 3, 1

In similar imagery is Prospero's reflexion on the mutability of all things, which fade like Ceres' pageant. Allegory is a fabric of Inverse Metaphor. For some time after the decline of allegorical composition Inverse Metaphor appeared infrequently in English poetry. Wordsworth's listening ear for nature signalizes in this respect a new order. The Direct Metaphor shows the poet at home in his art, less conventional and nearer to the ways of our symbol-making thought. As a dominating feature in literature and in literal experience it may place nature above man, and subjugate initiative and will. This might be considered the case in the tragedies of the four modern dramatists whom I have just mentioned.

A final type of metaphor not appearing in the rhetorical categories is the Implied Image. An instance in which there is considerable room for doubt is the most valuable from the standpoint of definition. Take the opening phrase in a poet of supreme power as an imagist. In Pindar's favorite words "now if water be the best" there appears to me a touchstone of the simplicity, clarity, sweetness and austerity of the Greek heroic ideal. Whether such is the poet's intention or not, this interpretation readily illustrates the type of Implied Imagery, an unknown quantity in the categories of the rhetoricians.

Since the rhetorical categories are not to be employed in this essay it may be asked on what basis the investigation will be pursued. An effort will be made to determine the imaginative value of metaphors selected from Elizabethan literature, to assign the causes for their position, and to examine the larger groups of figures as they appear on an ascending scale from the lowest, or most nearly literal, to the most imaginative, or impressionistic. This scheme is purely descriptive. The furthest departure from literal statement may be found in an image essentially false or ludicrously misplaced. It may occur in such opulent and exuberant figures as those of Burke censured by Matthew

Arnold. Metaphor may be thought of as a tool. A great hammer is useless in mending a fine piece of machinery. Imagery which may be admired in the impassioned themes of Marlowe would be out of place in the sober themes of "the well-languaged" Daniel. By the question whether this or that imagery is better adapted to its end, or whether one end is higher than another, we are not affected. We are concerned only in describing what the mind does when it takes the leap of metaphor; whether it skips in a delicate conceit or places us for the moment on an imaginative elevation. The present theme is to describe poetic metaphor. The character and degree of imaginative activity are the sole points of inquiry. It may be expected that the reader will form on the basis of such a study ethical judgments and preferences in taste. These, to reiterate, are left so far as possible unprejudiced in my presentation.

The figures lowest on the scale of imaginative activity though to be dismissed from our discussion are not to be dismissed as unprofitable. They belong to one of the most useful of the categories, rarely found in verse but frequent in scientific writing. To criticize them is to refine the distinction between the metaphorical comparison and poetic metaphor. They should be observed as the basis and negative starting point of all ensuing distinctions. They are of the type of imagery usually found in scientific terminology. For illustrations of the metaphor of poetry it may be convenient to turn to Elizabethan literature. Illustrations of the metaphor of science are no more abundant in an historical study. This image is neutral while the poetic image is sympathetic. One is purely descriptive; the other has a subjective value. "Pup tent" in military language is a poetic metaphor. The figure not only describes roughly the size and appearance of the tent, but expresses in a humorous epithet something of what the soldier thinks of life in such a house. The poetic image has an emotional and richly imaginative value, leaving its subject nobler, more delightful or more abhorred. The image of science on the other hand appeals to the calculating and descriptive faculty, leaving its subject more vivid, more memorable, more accurately perceived and still without disproportionate emphasis. Consider an ideal metaphor in the terminology of science. "Styleline," or little pen, is a small and extinct species of pteropod which because of its general form and a slit commonly found near the point resembles a pen. This term is memorable, accurate and restrained. It may be contrasted with the word "crocodilus," derived from roots signifying pebbly and vile. The animal, with reference to its skin, is figuratively called "a vile pebbly thing." This was somewhat too picturesque a term for science in Greece. It is now cumbersome and literal. A poetic figure has become a faded figure. Unfortunate metaphorical terms are notable in Grammar, as for example "strong" and "weak" of adjectives, "masculine" and "feminine" of nouns, and the conception of a verb "governing" its object. These are apparently survivals of a medieval allegorical terminology. Words that depreciate or commend by metaphor are undesirable for scientific use. "Yellow" union is of this sort. "Pudding stone" is too sensational language for the scientist, who speaks of conglomerates. No objection however can be brought against the term styleline. It holds the mind of the scientist within his laboratory. It is accurate and memorable. For scientific terminology nothing more can be desired. What is an excellent metaphor here is worthless as poetic imagery.

"A simile," says Johnson in his *Life of Pope*, "to be perfect must both illustrate and ennoble its subject; must show it to the understanding in a clearer view, and display it to the fancy with greater dignity; but either of these qualities may be sufficient to recommend it." One may consider it admirable moderation in Johnson to place his highest commendation on figures that share the two qualities. Although exuberant imagery is farthest removed from the metaphorical comparison, it may not commend itself so thoroughly as a less diffused form. An ideal figure, it may be assumed, is one which appeals strongly to the imagination without offending the judgment. Such are the images of reflection, whether in the mouth of Shakespere's Edgar or of Francis Bacon.

Poetic metaphor in Elizabethan literature will be treated under several heads. Since each category will be viewed in contrast with others, and the entire series as an increasing departure from the neutral comparison, it is necessary to prefix a general summary of the scheme.

The Decorative Image is characterized by the greatest restriction of imagination. This restriction appears in pastoral conceits, which are the cool extravagancies of ingenuity, and in conventional figures depreciated like a popular tune through familiarity and trivial association. Manifest absurdities never appealing to the deeper imagination appear in pathetic fallacies, the decorative hyperbole and fantastic personifications. Diminutives artfully belittle the value of the substance of a poem, which declines still further when the interest passes from the major to the minor terms of the figures. The more such images are massed the slighter they become. The Decorative Image may indicate a frank trifling, or just fail to hide under artificial forms a real affection, cynicism or distress. One may not always know whether it is mirth that speaks or sorrow in mirth's language. The form is typically Elizabethan. These figures will for the present suffice to illustrate it.

> O, if the streets were paved with thine eyes,
> Her feet were much too dainty for such tread.
>
> *L. L. L.* IV, 3, 278

> Hasting to raunch the arrow out,
>   Hey ho Perigot,
> I left the head in my heart root;
>   It was a desperate shot!
>
> Sp. *S. C.* VII, 112

> Loitering live you little herdgrooms
> Keeping your beasts in the budded brooms.
>
> Sp. *S. C.* II, 35

The Sunken Image occurs where the metaphor is obscured. Although a metaphorical meaning is indicated, no definite picture is called to mind. Samuel Daniel excelled in the form. It may be equally congenial to a classical and a romantic taste. Much of the vigor and fascination of Shakespere's language is due to his immense vocabulary of hinted metaphor. The following image from Daniel was quoted with warm acknowledgment by Wordsworth, another master of the type:

> unless above himself he can
> *Erect* himself, how poor a thing is man!
>
> *To the Countess of Cumberland*

It is Chapman who writes:

> I am put off from this dull shore of ease
> Into *industrious* and high-going seas.
>
> *Byron's Conspiracy,* II, 1, 149

Violent Imagery, or the figure of Fustian, is a harsh and sensational form of metaphorical hyperbole that takes the mind by shock. It is without originality, subtlety or accuracy, and is unaccompanied by beauty, delicacy or meditation. This is the melodrama of metaphor, where less is meant than meets the ear. By the end of the sixteenth century the more naïve and cruder forms of fustian, associated in particular with the early stage, were much on the decline. Somewhat similar imagery appears in the Heroic Drama of the Restoration, and is perennial in sen-

sational story, journalism and speech making.   This is an
Elizabethan image of blood, thunder and thrill:

> Ere Arthur lands the sea shall blush with blood,
> And all the strands with smoking slaughter reek!
>
> *The Misfortunes of Arthur*, I, 4, 124

Radical imagery occurs where two terms of a metaphor
meet on a limited ground, and are otherwise definitely incongruent.   It makes daring excursions into the seemingly
commonplace.   The minor term promises little imaginative
value.   In a coldness to apparently incongruent suggestion
this figure approaches the neutral comparison, while in ingenuity it approaches the conceit.   A robust strength and
a powerful though narrow application, as well as its association with serious thought, lift it however to no mean
rank on the scale of imaginative values.   In the masterly
hands of Donne it becomes a vehicle for introspection, passion and ideas.   One of his best known figures concerns
love, absence and a pair of compasses:

> Our two souls therefore, which are one,
>   Though I must go, endure not yet
> A breach, but an expansion,
>   Like gold to airy thinness beat.
>
> If they be two, they are two so
>   As stiff twin compasses are two;
> Thy soul, the fix'd foot, makes no show
>   To move, but doth, if th' other do.
>
> And though it in the center sit,
>   Yet, when the other far doth roam,
> It leans, and hearkens after it,
>   And grows erect as that comes home.
>
> So wilt thou be to me, who must,
>   Like th' other foot, obliquely run;
> Thy firmness makes my circle just,
>   And makes me end where I begun.
>
> *A Valediction Against Mourning*

Here are a familiar Radical image from Shakespere, and a powerful example from Fulke Greville:

> And almost thence my nature is subdued
> To what it works in, like the dyer's hand.
>
> *Son.* 111

> Then man, endure thyself; these clouds will vanish;
> Life is a top which whipping sorrow driveth.
>
> *Caelica,* 87

The Intensive Image is associated with ritual and the pictorial arts, characterized in its minor term by dignity, conventionality, beauty and clarity, and affords intense though often impalpable suggestions. In beauty, conventionality and dignity it is distinguished from the Radical form. Restriction in scope especially distinguishes it from Expansive and Exuberant figures, the minor terms of which are drawn from wide excursions of the imagination. In this figure there is little or no emphasis upon magnitude. It appears in emblems, personifications, pageantry and ceremony. It is characteristic of the painters, priests and poets whose adorations have been more poignant and intense than glowing or sublime. The Intensive imagist finds something more divine than sublimity. Dante, Petrarch and Spenser express themselves more typically in this form; Homer, Shakespere and Milton in the Expansive Image. The form culminates in chastened and refined figures of ritualistic religion and idealism. The restraint in the following instances may be especially observed.

> The blue in black, the green in gray is tinct.
>
> Sp. *S. C.* XI

> On Fame's eternal beadroll worthy to be filed.
>
> Sp. *F. Q.* IV, 2, 32

> O goodly golden chain wherewith yfere
> The virtues linked are in lovely wise.
>
> Ib. I, 9, 1

The Muses that were wont green bays to wear
Now bringen bitter elder branches sere.
> Ib. *S. C.* XI

The fairest flower our girlond all among
Is faded quite and into dust ygo.
> Ib. *S. C.* XI

There's rosemary, that's for remembrance; pray love,
remember; and there is pansies, that's for thoughts.
> *Ham.* IV, 5, 175

Those crystal fingers dealing heavenly alms
Give all the wealth of all the world away.
> Drayton, *Muses Elyzium,* V

Expansive Imagery is characterized by the unloosing of a wide range of suggestion, and the strong and mutual modification of its parts. It appears equally in emotional and reflective poetry. Its figures may evoke beauty or terror. It is the figure of expansive energy. Some of its metaphors are in full and eloquent language; others cram into a pregnant word a wealth of suggestion. The physical picture passes beyond any restricted frame of time or space. Sometimes there is a league of imagination and fancy in which imagination still holds the ascendency. The form culminates in those comprehensive metaphors of philosophy and religion represented in Burke, in *The Advancement of Learning* and in the *Religio Medici.* To this category belong the larger number of the images cited from Shakespere. It is the imagery of Isaiah and the Iconoclasts, as the Intensive figure belongs rather to Dante and the Catholic mind. These figures are representative of the Expansive category.

> beauty's ensign yet
> Is crimson in thy lips and in thy cheeks,
> And death's pale flag is not advanced there.
> > *Rom. and Jul.* V, 3, 94

O Spartan dog,
More fell than anguish, hunger or the sea.
Oth. V, 2, 362

But thy eternal summer shall not fade.
Son. 18

O, he smiles valiantly.
Does he not?
O yes, an't were a cloud in autumn.
T. and C. I, 2, 137

When you do dance, I wish you
A wave o' the sea, that you might ever do
Nothing but that.
W. T. IV, 4, 140

That this huge stage presenth naught but shows
Whereon the stars in secret influence comment.
Son. 15

There is surely a piece of divinity in us; something
that was before the elements and owes no homage to the sun.
Browne, *Religio Medici,* II, 11

The Exuberant Image is characterized by energetic impressionism. Two powerfully imaginative terms influence one another strongly, while their relation remains vague and indefinite. A common loveliness for example may alone associate the ideas. Here occur metaphorical protestations of worth, and hyperbole of the highest imaginative value. The five senses are confused in intoxicating imagery. The form readily passes into animism and the supernatural. In Exuberant Imagery Homer likens the child of Andromache to a star. To such imagery Drayton seems to have referred when he praised the earlier of the great Elizabethan poets for "brave translunary things." Marlowe is its ideal representative. Variations of the form may be found in the poetry of religious enthusiasm, in *The Song of Songs.* There are abundant Exuberant images in the poetry of Francis Thompson. It may be illustrated in another phase from the love songs of Burns. Some may condemn it as "Asiatic," others may extol it as sublime. These are illustrations:

> O thou art fairer than the evening air
> Clad in the beauty of a thousand stars!
>> Marlowe, *Dr. Faustus,* XIII, 104

> If heaven would make me such another world
> Of one entire and perfect chrysolite
> I'd not have sold her for it.
>> *Oth.* V, 2, 144

> There's not the smallest orb which thou beholdst
> But in his motions like an angel sings,
> Still quiring to the young ey'd cherubins.
>> *M. V.* V, I, 60

> Eternity was in our lips and eyes.
>> *Ant. and Cleo.* I, 3, 35

The imagery of wit and humor may be considered as a supplement to these seven categories. Its figures are too diversified to admit a general definition. They may be observed as variations on the preceding forms. Images of wit suggest the Decorative and Radical figures, but are often more resonant in their imaginative value. Images of humor suggest the Expansive category, but are generally far fetched and extravagant. A humorous fancy may animate what would otherwise be a conceit, or attenuate what might readily be an Expansive metaphor. The sharpened images of intellectual wit and irony are relatively rare in Elizabethan literature. Those drawn from fairylike fancy on the one hand and from the grotesque gothic humor of the tavern on the other are brought in writers like Day and Nash to a high degree of excellence. This humor is nearer to poetry than to criticism, and to song than to satire.

Typical of gothic humor are Falstaff's almost Miltonic images on Bardolph's nose, now glowing in the darkness like
the light of a man of war, in fog and storm, now like a
memento of infernal fires.

No writer confines himself to but one of these types of
metaphor, though only a few, with Shakespere, supply illustrations of them all. Some authors however are eminent in a single form. A preliminary survey of the categories will be assisted if one associated Sidney with the
Decorative, Daniel with the Sunken, Kyd with the Violent,
Donne with the Radical, Spenser with the Intensive, Bacon
with the Expansive, Marlowe with the Exuberant and Nash
with the Humorous forms. These categories do not represent a comprehensive view of Elizabethan Imagery. They
do however represent the chief tendencies in the metaphorical imagination of the period. Indeed there are few tendencies in poetic metaphor which are not found in this age.

The value of such a study as the one here undertaken
cannot lie in the definition of a number of types of metaphor. Definition is a means to an end. The purpose of
establishing a type of metaphor is to illustrate the character of individuals, the culture of an age, and the potentiali-
ties of metaphorical thought. A study of poetic imagery
is an unfrequented path that reveals from new angles the
moral, intellectual and aesthetic life of a poet and his times.
From the purely technical study of metaphorical types, for
example, we gain fresh evidence on the garrulous and
platitudinous mind of Lyly; on the sober mind of Daniel;
on the vigorous but coarse and sensational nature of Kyd;
on the passionate, analytical and introspective nature of
Donne; on the intense idealism and the conservatism of
Spenser; on the intellectual grasp and daring and eloquence of Bacon; on the exuberant Helicon of Marlowe;
and on the abundant poetic humor of Thomas Nash. The
valiancy and fantastic aspiration of the Elizabethan age

itself appear in the mere technique of an imagery which transfigures the most vulgar object at the touch of poetry, and makes the perilous circle of the globe on the wings of metaphor. When it is difficult to form a judgment from a mass of evidence, a mannerism may give the desired clue. So narrow and precise a rule as metaphorical study affords may still be of assistance in measuring the minds and hearts of men.

II

THE DECORATIVE IMAGE

The Decorative Image is one in which the two terms are as incongruent as metaphor will allow, and so constituted and associated that the imaginative values are reduced to a minimum. The idea of incongruity suggests the Radical figure. In the case of the Radical image however one term in what is otherwise an ingenious relation has a strong poetic value, and the total effect is to arouse and to direct the imagination, not to deaden and disperse it. The most important conception in Decorative imagery is incongruity. In a more sympathetic figure the minor term is interpretative. Thus the entire metaphor resembles a Greek statue with formal drapery that makes the body itself more eloquent. The minor term in Decorative imagery might be compared to an ear-ring which hangs with dangling irrelevancy from its dedicated object. The art of this imagery is the exotic and illogical art of gingerbread ornamentation. For this conception of structural irrelevancy and incongruity there is no practicable exposition beyond the review of examples one by one. A considerably larger number of figures in this Chapter than in succeeding ones will accordingly be examined from the somewhat dry standpoint of definition. The test of incongruity is, to be sure, a simple one. It is that literal-minded test with which Samuel Johnson met every image. With the conception of imaginative values on the contrary there is room for much criticism and development, as well as for disagreement in the application of general conclusions. I shall illustrate how imaginative value is reduced in the Decorative figure by the essential incongruity of the form, by improbability, conventionality, particularization, confusion, or by use of the diminutive. Sometimes the minor term is reduced by the major, sometimes the major by the minor. In examining all figures one should inquire first why they are as incongruent as metaphor will allow, and second why they fail to stimulate the higher imagination.

The first group of figures, three in number, is comprised of images in which a minor term with a promise of imaginative value is reduced to a minimum by contact with a major term. Spenser says of a ram,

> His horns be as broad as rainbow bent.
>
> *S. C.* II, 80

The first question concerns the incongruity of the figure. We may speak of the horns of the rainbow. Consequently in spite of the rather literal-minded process we make out of the line a metaphor. The terms are nearly unsympathetic and certainly incongruous. In the second place we inquire whether either of the terms possesses imaginative fullness or intensity. The ram's horns are not here the objects of great admiration. From the earliest poetry to Wordsworth however the rainbow has been regarded as an object of extreme beauty and awesomeness. When Shakespere's Ceres calls it the "rich scarf to my proud earth," fancy creates an ideal being to wear the rainbow as a delicate adornment. Though the fancy is bold, there is no incongruity, nor as the scarf to a fruitful world does the rainbow undergo an indignity. The metaphor that includes the ram's horns on the contrary is a masterpiece of poetic bathos. The pastoral poet affecting the ram, admiring the rainbow and disregarding "natural piety," associates rainbow and ram by discrete impudence and calculated audacity. He adorns his verse with the pleasant suggestion of a rainbow, but reduces the imaginative value of the figure to the lowest possible degree.

Consider another figure of the same type.   This shepherd
is distressed:

> My ragged ronts all shiver and shake
> As doen high towers in an earthquake.
>
> *S. C.* II, 5

The shepherd's limbs are shaking, and so do towers in an
earthquake.   There is a perceptible metaphor.   The incongruity consists in comparing an unreal shepherd shivering
in an unreal February to the terrors of mankind in the
most dreadful of catastrophes.   Although the terms are in
a somewhat prosaic relation, one of them is too imaginative to allow the figure to fall under the category of the
non-poetic metaphor or the metaphor of science.   When
however an earthquake is associated with such a shivering
shepherd, it awes no one.

A further illustration of the type may be taken from
Browne's Britannia's Pastorals:

> The striken swain lean'd to a tree
> As void of sense as weeping Niobe.
>
> I, 1, 41

A metaphorical element appears in the comparison of con-
sternation and a thunderstroke.   The metaphor is a desperate hyperbole.   What could be more incongruous than a
comparison of what is stricken by thunder to a conventional shepherd who after some hard luck in love leans his
back against a forest tree?   When Lear witnesses that the
thunder would not "peace" at his bidding, the idea becomes powerful in poetic imagery.   When associated with
the swain in Britannia's Pastorals thunder ceases to alarm,
and is not intended to alarm.   As a general summary of
the type presented in these three images one observes that
by reducing to the level of pastoral verse the terrors of
thunder and earthquake and the sublimity of the rainbow,
and deriving a pastoral sentiment, a chill and a ram's

horns, not only have the phenomena of nature suffered, but the pastoral world itself has undergone a still further degradation. One feature has been made smaller still by holding above the entire world a diminishing glass. All the stars and the frame of things are reduced through metaphor to a cosmos of triviality. In tragic poetry on the contrary our world of mediocrity is transfigured through metaphor into a universe of indisputable dignity. August and sublime concepts, as in a Feast of Fools, suffer the indignity of pastoral verse. The swain's sorrows are not lifted to the thunder, but the thunder is reduced to the swain's sorrows, which in turn pass out of all appreciable significance. Intrinsically the terms in these figures have no mutually sympathetic relation. Thus far they resemble the metaphor of science, and not the poetic figure. They have however an aesthetic relation influencing one another in a sophisticated progression, as the terms in a declining ratio. They may be considered as the lowest and most freakish form of poetic metaphor.

The next group shows the same tendency of a poetic idea to suffer in association with a slight or prosaic one. But what is formally the reverse takes place. The major term is reduced in value by the minor term. In the preceding figures a world of rams, chills and sentiments was nominally illustrated by conceptions of the rainbow, earthquake and thunderings, with the belittling of the latter as a notable result. In the following figures a world of storms, stars, fears, heartlessness and loyalty is diminished by nominal comparisons to bowls of broth, groats, stilt-walking, painted fires and spaniels. The first of these images is from *The Merchant of Venice*.

> My wind cooling my broth
> Would blow me to an ague when I thought
> What harm a wind too great at sea might do.
>
> I, 1, 22

There is enough of a relation between a tempest on the ocean and a tempest in a bowl of broth to make metaphor. It is poetic metaphor not because it is directly sympathetic but because it is perverse. A storm at sea is a serious affair; but a tempest in a bowl of broth is a tempest in a teapot. The association of the two ideas makes the storm at sea laughable and the emotional and imaginative value of the tempest in the broth infinitesimal. Two further points may be observed in this figure. It is in the rhetorical sense neither a metaphor nor a simile, though in the present terminology it is a Direct metaphor. And a merchant so sensitive as to be frightened into an ague while calmly blowing his broth would certainly break under the strain of the Exchange. But Salarino is not reported to have failed. The dilemma is not difficult. He was innocently affecting the whimsies of a gentleman. He experienced no such ague. The warning is not to take an Elizabethan conceitist at his word. He had a tough heart beneath his fantastic cloak.

In *Astrophel and Stella* occurs the following image:

> Desire still on the stilts of fear doth go.
>
> Song 8

There is just a sufficient thread of metaphor between the fears of a lover and the timidity of a stilt-walker to make imagery. Though it is curious enough to be a poetic metaphor it is nothing better than ingenious. In the lyric from which this figure is taken, the climax of Sidney's Stella poems, there is much genuine feeling. The verses thoroughly transmit the lover's fear. Whether or not the fear is derivable from this quaint and ingenious image is a matter of personal reaction. In my own reading the metaphor reduces the serious import of the lines. Meeting it in Donne one would probably feel otherwise.

These lines are also from Sidney:

The welkin had full nigardly inclosed
In coffer of dim clouds his silver groats.

Arcadia, I, 90

By a freak of fancy an overcast sky may be thought of as
a miser of the stars. Yet the clues are small for building
such an image. It is evidently a metaphor of wit, ingenious and conceited. In the second place we ask if either of
the terms is imaginatively conceived and if the imaginative
term is reduced by the association. The potency of the
stars is certainly diminished in this metaphor. If to men
of the world groats seem more valuable than stars, in
poetry we assume the stars more significant than groats.
In Jonson's *Volpone* coins might receive from his poetic
miser a benefit from the stars. So might the coins in the
hoard of the Jew of Malta. But in Sidney the stars are
only diminished to the significance of silver coins.

Campion has written that

Women's hearts are painted fires.

I, 4

This figure has perhaps more of the typical characteristics
of poetic metaphor than any of the preceding. The contrast of a warm and living flame to a cold and motionless
representation of that flame on canvas is by no means without subtlety. Ingenious however it assuredly is. One
feels that this kind of cold and intellectual love poetry is
itself admirably illustrated in Campion's painted flames.
Here is nothing to indicate that the author derives more
ardor from living than from painted fires. The level of
feeling is definitely reduced by the nature of the image.

A further illustration of the same type may be taken
from the *Arcadia.* "O that I might well, like a spaniel,
gnaw upon the chain that ties him!" This may be considered a metaphor since the idea of a spaniel gnawing his
chain is associated, however slenderly, with the idea of of-

fering release. The association of the lover and the spaniel is far fetched enough to comply with the requirement of
incongruity in the Decorative image. A depreciation in
sympathy is inevitable in such a figure.

The major term in the following image refers not to a
thought or feeling but to nature.

> A hill that holds his head, as though he told a tale,
> Or stooped to look down or whisper to a vale.
>
> Drayton, *Poly-Olbion*, XX, 271

The conception of an overleaning hill as a stooping figure
may be regarded as metaphor. The idea is also far fetched
and depreciated. The hill becomes a loquacious old story
teller. One fancies that like Drayton it may be full of old
Dodonian tales; but no very serious tales are to be expected
which are introduced in so fantastic a fashion. The idea
of the tale teller reduces the imaginative value of the mountain to the level of pastoral imagination.

In all the preceding figures ideas of considerable imaginative value have perversely been diminished by unexpected conjunction with the commonplace or the fantastical. In the four images which are to follow none of the
terms has a comparable promise. Incongruity is not so
great, but still perceptible.

> As if it should stand there like a hand in the margin of a
> book to note some saying worthy to be marked.
>
> *Arcadia,* I, 90

> To trim his thick boughs in the crystal brook.
>
> Browne, *Britannia's Pastorals,*
> II, 2, 60

> When she embarked did you not mark how the winds whistled
> for joy?
>
> *Arcadia,* I, 2

> (His hair) was stirred up and down with the wind which
> seemed to have sport to play with it, as the sea had to kiss his
> feet.
>
> *Arcadia,* I, 4

The figure of a hand in a margin is "pedantical" and insignificant. That of boughs trimming themselves over the water is graceful but in no high degree sympathetic. The iteration of these arboreal toilets in pastoral poetry deadens whatever element of fancy the figure may originally have contained. Much the same may be said of Sidney's whistling winds and caressing waves. These images are conspicuous as metaphorical excrescences.

The characteristic of incongruity is not the only one which reduces the imaginative value of the Decorative image. The pastoral poets not only oppose objects and abstractions which are in themselves far fetched and incongruous but remake nature to their hearts' desire. The physical improbability of their images frequently compels one to take their verse lightly. Campion says of the teeth of his mistress, "They looked like rose-buds filled with snow." Traversing once more the ground of our definition we ask first, do teeth in a lady's mouth look anything like snow? Answering that they do we conclude the line a metaphor; and hastily adding that they do not look much like snow in a rose-bud, we find that thus far the image is Decorative. There is the requisite incongruity. Contrasted with most of the previous illustrations the depreciation in this figure is less marked. A new characteristic however gives assurance of the slightness of the poet's imagination. A rose-bud filled with snow is a delectable improbability. We, who suffer and are glad not as the poet wills but as nature wills, regard verses in which nature is manipulated to his whim as delicately inconsequential.

This artificial device takes numerous colors, as may appear from a few citations.

> Betwixt their crystal arms they clip that loved place.
> *Poly-Olbion,* III, 84

The artful coolness and ingenuity in the conception of the chaste embraces of the stream is still further removed into an artificial world by the epithet "crystal." In the *Shepherd's Calendar* we read:

> And he that strives to touch the stars
> Oft stumbles at a straw.

VII, 106

This again, though the conceit may have been a popular saw, shows all the marks of calculated ingenuity. A diminution of sympathetic imagination is assured by the abrupt turn of the figure from stars to straw. But men neither touch the stars nor stumble over straws. The impossibility of the figure as well as the absurd contrast compels a low imaginative value. In *Love's Labor's Lost* Shakespere writes:

> O if the streets were paved with thine eyes,
> Her feet were much too dainty for such tread!

IV, 3, 278

The metaphor consists in the idea that to tread upon is to disgrace. This idea is complicated by a wild improbability, the conception of a lover's eyes as a pavement for his love. To presume such a world is to lower the passage into an atmosphere in which the finer imaginative faculties cannot live. Sidney's metaphorical mind seldom took a wilder leap than when he wrote: "Her eyes are more pleasant to behold than two white kids climbing up a fair tree." If this can be taken as metaphor at all, it generously complies with the Decorative requirement of incongruity. Kids are animals about whom the readers of sophisticated pastoral poetry may be presumed to know and seriously to care little. The value of the figure then is sufficiently diminished. In addition, however, we have the preposterous notion of two white kids climbing a fair tree. The image is farcical. As a final illustration of the Decorative world of simple improbability one of the most familiar of all conceits may be cited. It is instanced in Spenser:

> Hasting to raunch the arrow out,
> Hey ho Perigot,
> I left the head in my heart root;
> It was a desperate shot!

The surgical improbability of this conceit is of the extraordinary world of Decorative verse.

Associated with figures of simple improbability is the type of the "pathetic fallacy." This is an animistic image in skeptical and sophisticated thought. When animism is powerful enough to force a suspension of disbelief, as in the instance of the rocks that sensitive to beauty let Othello's bride go by, there is, in my use of the word, no trace of the pathetic fallacy. Neither is this Decorative imagery. There is no pathetic fallacy in an illusion of life in a humming dynamo. The pathetic fallacy occurs when animistic imagery is the frank assumption of Decorative poetry, a conscious and highly artificial device, subverting the stronger imagination. If the idea of an animistic image is not only artificial, but if the animated object is made to act in an unnatural manner, a still further descent is taken on the scale of imaginative values. Personification and animism, it should be added, are not in themselves metaphor. They become metaphorical when the form or action of the personified figure is descriptive of the associated idea, or when the animated object is conceived to possess a spirit metaphorically corresponding to its semblance.

These figures not only illustrate the pathetic fallacy but the vagaries of a newly animated world:

> The fishes in the flood
> When she doth angle
> For the hook strive a-good
> Them to entangle;
> And leaping on the land

From the clear water,
Their scales upon the sand
Lavishly scatter,
Therewith to pave the mold
Whereon she passes,
So herself to behold
As in her glasses.
Drayton, *Shepherd's Sirena*

(of sheep)
Whose hanging heads did seem his dreary case to weep.
Sp. *S. C.* I, 36

For brass or marble were they seated here
Would fret or melt in tears to lie so near.
Browne, *Britannia's Pastorals,* II, 4, 561

Why slide these brooks so slow away
Whose bubbling murmur pleased thy ear?
O marvel not although they stay
When they her heavenly music hear!
Drayton, *Shepherd's Garland*

Fishes, sheep, marble and brooks act here in quite a different fashion from that which the semblance of these animals and things suggests. Fishes are not more obsequious lovers of shepherdesses than shepherds themselves. Sheep are not to be expected to weep for their masters' wrongs. Marble would not generally be imagined to melt with passion, nor brooks to change their pace for a mortal song. Since Ruskin no form of Decorative imagery has met with less critical leniency than the pathetic fallacy. Yet a slight inspiration may perhaps be attributed to it. The venerable image of sympathetic sheep for example has given genial inspiration to at least one mind, as appears in the naïve wood cuts in the first edition of *The Shepherd's Calendar.*

If the underlying symbolism of the diminutive in *Gulliver's Travels* makes all that it touches mean, the cool and the slighting effect of the underlying diminutive in Decorative verse is equally symbolical. Here, then, is another means of reducing the imaginative value of the metaphors as well as the general significance of Decorative poetry. This is no formal test. Small articles, as handkerchiefs, have their part in tragedy. The tendency of Intensive imagery, as in Spenser, is to reduce the mere bulk of its objects. It is nevertheless worth noting how irresistibly we visualize the lesser pastoral world in diminutive form. Shepherds and shepherdesses were often no more than china dolls for the diversion of the generally grave courtiers of Queen Elizabeth. Drayton's *Nymphidia* is an epic of the little people; Spenser's *Muipotmos* and his *Virgil's Gnat* are like insect painting. A typical diminutive with Decorative effect may be taken from *The Shepherd's Calendar*. Aged Thenot prudentially warns a diminutive Cuddie that life's wintry frowns wait on idleness.

> Loitering live you little herdgrooms
> Keeping your beasts in the budded brooms . . .
> Then pay you the price of your surquedry
> With weeping and wailing and misery.
>
> II, 55

This diminutive helps one to take Thenot's counsel with a grain of salt. In the same way the typical images and personifications in Decorative poetry when cast in the diminutive make the precepts and passions fall more lightly on head and heart. The convention of the nightingale, in Sidney's words "a thorn her song-book making," is a typical emblem for the lover's woes. Cupid is a tiny god from whom in decorative verse no serious wounds are to be feared. Among the Elizabethan conventions of the melancholy nightingale tilted against a briar, few are daintier than Barnfield's popular song. Among the personifications of Cupid few are so charming as that in the last two lines of Campion's song to cold-hearted ladies. These figures beside illustrating the Decorative diminutive show how fresh the most conventional images may become when handled with a touch of genius.

> Everything did banish moan
> Save the nightingale alone.
> She, poor bird, as all forlorn
> Leaned her breast against a thorn.
> Fie, fie, fie now she would cry,
> Teru, teru, by and by,
> That to hear her so complain
> Scarce I could from tears refrain.
>
> *England's Helicon,* 66

> But in their breasts where love his court should hold
> Poor Cupid sits and blows his nails for cold.
>
> *Campion,* I, 4

More important than the diminutive and more directly related to the definition of metaphor is a tendency to particularization or minute description. Decorative imagery describes the throat, the cheeks, the hair, the beauty "of hand, of foot, of lip, of eye, of brow." These descriptive images pass as a current but by no means precious coinage between lovers. Long established convention has worn them from the freshness of flowers in the field to the polish of flowers in glass. There is a good reason for the restriction of theme in such Decorative figures. The more a figure comprehends, the greater is as a rule the call upon the imagination. The Decorative image is the least comprehensive of all the forms of poetic metaphor. Contrast aids illustration. Marlow's Faustus exclaims:

> O thou art fairer than the evening air
> Clad in the beauty of a thousand stars!

Here is an Exuberant metaphor likening the entirety of Helen's beauty to the beauty of the night. The same type of imagination appears in Burns' familiar song:

> My love is like a red, red rose
> That's newly sprung in June!
> My love is like a melody
> That's sweetly played in tune!

On the contrary the metaphor in society verse likens only the lips of the shepherdess to the rose, or her voice to the music of a bird. Such particularization is the reverse of high imaginative activity. Even as metaphor the descriptive comparisons of Decorative verse are under suspicion. The reader will recall the distinction between the comparison and the poetic metaphor. To call the sea as grey as lead or to think a cloud a whale is not poetic metaphor, but comparison. Such figures are deficient in the requisite subjective element. The value in Decorative poetry of the pearl and the cowslip as metaphor lies not in the comparison of the pearl to the pale white of the neck, nor in the comparison of the cowslip to the gold of the hair, but in a small share of that eternal metaphor which brings beauty to love.

The descriptive Decorative convention, then, is diminished in imaginative value through particularization and weak metaphorical power. It is frequently allied not only with the improbable but with the artificial. It has never been the custom for example to paint the human face in the bold colors which Decorative imagery prescribes. An extreme artificiality in the Intensive image often produces to be sure a profound imaginative effect. Angels with golden faces dive like bees into the rose of the *Paradiso*. The artificialities of Dante's mystic vision however have a far different function from the conventional artificialities in Decorative poetry. Beauty is in the latter reduced to its lowest terms. These delicate figures please but do not delight. They are distinguished from higher forms of imagery as the trinket from the gem. The artificiality of the Decorative images typical of such an anthology of pastoral verse as *England's Helicon,* and the artificiality of the Intensive images typical of *The Fairie Queene* illustrate two extremes on a single line of progression. The colors which the poet lays on his figures by means of metaphor introduce the critic to the field of painting. The distinction of the two styles is of course best observable there. Here however are some artificial Decorative figures in a charming stanza from Campion's *Airs.* Beside them may be placed the lines of the mechanical Thisbe in *A Midsummer-Night's Dream,* which gently profane the conventional ideas.

> All you that will hold watch with love,
>   The Fairy Queen Perserpina
> Will make you fairer than Dian's dove;
>   Roses red, lilies white,
> And the clear damask hue
>   Shall on your cheeks alight.
> Love will adorn you.
>
> *Campion,* I, 2

> These lily lips,
> This cherry nose,
> These yellow cowslip cheeks!
>
> *M. S. N. D.* V, 337

The survey of Decorative imagery suggested in the preliminary definition is now complete.

At this point however a few more of the transitional forms may be cited, as well as a few of those figures in other categories which suggest the present.

The typical image of fancy shows ingenuity without depreciation. It is therefore related to the Decorative form and distinguishable from it. Consider as an illustration of pure fancy Shakespere's line, "Cowslips tall her pensioners be." This image might seem to the literal-minded reader almost arbitrary. It is cast in the diminutive. Thus far it is true to the Decorative type. Imaginative vigor is however by no means depreciated. Even from the standpoint of incongruity the figure is bold, not calculated. The Decorative image is the result of conscious ingenuity. Pedantical is its epithet and Holofernes its professor. All figures in this category are far fetched, though most are time-worn and conventional. Such are the typical images in *Love's Labor's Lost*. The figures of creative fancy are best represented in *A Midsummer-Night's Dream*. They are free from straitened tradition, unencumbered by laborious effort, liberated from hair-splitting ingenuity and winged with bird-like daring. Their notes though slender and fine retain a silvery resonance. An image in Decorative poetry pleases like the witticism of a moment. To delight continuously without fatigue is the first characteristic of an image of fancy. This form will be considered in connection with the Expansive figure. From the standpoint of imaginative activity the images of fancy cannot well be distinguished from those which bear the weight of the tragedy of Othello. The highest sphere is inhabited equally by the eagle and the lark. From the standpoint of imaginative activity however the pedantical decorative conceit and the winged metaphor of fancy are widely divergent. The intellectual figure startles with an apparently incongruous association. When the surprise passes the image is forgotten. The image of fancy is characterized by romantic suggestion, by mutual influence between the terms and by a freedom from the calculating spirit. It affords delight at what is unexpected but exquisitely appropriate. It is still fragrant when lost to the sight. The image of Queen Mab's cowslip pensioners is memorable for its audacity, its ineffable fitness and its fragrance. The intellect alone is invited to the somewhat childish task of discovering ingenious metaphor in the figures of the shivering shepherd and the earthquake, the ram's horns and the rainbow, the tempest in the broth and on the sea. In short

the Decorative image is justified by the intellect but preposterous to the imagination, while the image of fancy is
practically inexplicable to the intellect but justified by the
imagination.

Yet such theoretical explanation seems almost too clear,
for its application only reveals the precariousness of taste.
The following citations might be variously classified by
readers who subscribed to the same theoretical distinctions
between the two types. In my own reading of the six succeeding figures there is an ascent from a form tainted with
the manner of the conceit to the form of pure fancy. It
cannot be thought inappropriate to select as the consummate image of fancy a citation from Shelley.

. . . Is Toothy, tripping down from Verwin's rushy lair.
                    Drayton, *Poly-Olbion,* IV, 118

(of another stream)
Like a wanton girl oft doubling in her gait
In labyrinth like turns and twinings intricate.
                    Ib. XXII, 21

(of the marshes of Ouze)
As Amphitrite oft calls me her sweet and fair,
And sends the northern winds to curl my braided hair.
                    Ib. XX, 271

The frisking fairies then as on the light air born
Oft ran at barley break upon the ears of corn,
And catching drops of dew in their lascivious chases
Do cast the liquid pearl in one another's faces.
                    Ib. XXI, 97

(of fantasy)
Which is as thin of substance as the air,
And more inconstant than the wind, who wooes
Even now the frozen bosom of the north,
And, being angered, puffs away from thence,
Turning his face to the dew dropping south.
                    Rom. and Jul. I, 4, 99

> phials which shone
> In their own golden beams each like a flower,
> Out of whose depth a fire-fly shakes his light
> Upon a cypress, in a starless night.
>
> Shelley, *The Witch of Atlas,* **XX**

None of these figures possesses quite the inexplicable fitness which may be thought to belong to the cowslip pensioners.

Thus far the Decorative category has been described, and bounded in relation to others. It remains to illustrate its application and significance. Topics that merit attention under these heads are its application to serious verse, its relation to Decorative verse, its reliance on mass effect, and its tendency to what will be described as misaccent. In conclusion we may consider its history in Tudor literature and its significance in Elizabethan culture.

A characteristic of Decorative imagery is to elaborate without interpretation or serious adornment passages of gravity or imaginative pretension. This type, showing the slightest relation to its context, is most likely to fall under the censure of a modern critic. Something of the sort is to be seen in the figures of Lyly. It is perhaps most familiar in the scenes of counsel and debate in the Shakesperean Histories. The first act of *Henry Fifth* swarms with this national mannerism. The poet seems in possession of his full powers, but not of that mastery with which his powers are balanced in his mature art. In the First Part of *Henry Fourth* on the contrary the type of buoyant, Decorative imagery serves the artistic function of formal relief. Shakespere's tragedy itself is at times dressed in language that lies like a fantastically decorated cloak rising and falling under emotional stress. The imagery is subtly adapted to the scene. Thus the essential artificiality often remarked upon in the story of the first scene of *King Lear,* which is by all means a solemn scene, is fittingly cloaked in elaborate and Decorative metaphor. Although the speeches reveal emotion they are not themselves in that great language of emotion which is husbanded for the later scenes of the tragedy. Metaphor adapts itself to the development of the story. In *Antony and Cleopatra* the surface of imagery is often far more buoyant than the emotions which are intimated to lie beneath. Bubbles play about the brim. A gift for far-fetched metaphor is a part of that natural buoyancy by which Antony's delights

> Were dolphin like, they showed his back above
> The element they lived in.

This is a significant mood in Anglo-Saxon culture. By a delicate superstructure of trained expression thought is kept safe from the stagnation of sentimentality. Images of this type are of much greater psychological interest than their low value as poetic metaphor would suggest. Shakespere is the best source for such a study. A Euphuistic mannerism in his early work develops into a type of imagery which, whether we practice it to-day or not, does function in the ripest of his tragedies. Images incongruous in themselves are structural in relation to their context. These citations illustrate a progression.

> As many arrows, loosed several ways,
> Come to one mark; as many ways meet in one town;
> As many fresh streams meet in one salt sea;
> As many lines close in the dial's centre;
> So many thousand actions, once afoot,
> End in one purpose, and be all well borne
> Without defeat.
>
> *Hen. V,* I, 2, 207

> Will you again unknit
> This churlish knot of all-abhorred war?
>
> *I Hen. IV,* V, 1, 15

Yea, from the table of my memory
I'll wipe away all trivial fond records.
Ham. I, 5, 97

Thy bow is bent and drawn; make from the shaft.
Lear, I, 1, 145

to dismantle
So many folds of favor . . .
Lear, I, 1, 220

KENT My life I never held but as a pawn
To wage against thy enemies, ne'er fear to lose it,
Thy safety being motive.
Lear, I, 1, 157

CLEO. Prithee friend
Pour out the pack of matter to mine ear,
The good and bad together. He's friends with Caesar;
In state of health thou say'st; and thou say'st free.
Ant. and Cleo. II, 5, 53

Each of these figures appears more effective than its predecessor in stimulating that play of ingenuity in metaphor which glitters on the dark wave of tragedy. In the citation from *Henry Fifth* Shakespere follows Lyly, but in the citations from the tragedies, life. Many attitudes are possible toward the latter citations, but such imagery may not be dismissed as peculiarly a literary fad.

Although Decorative imagery appears in tragedy, it is intimately associated with a form of light verse which may also be called Decorative. Decorative poetry is highly artificial and conventional, expressing slender emotions and depicting a miniature world. Such are the "recreative" eclogues in *The Shepherd's Calendar,* Spenser's *Muipotmos* and his *Virgil's Gnat,* the larger part of *Love's Labor's Lost,* most of Sidney's *Arcadia,* most of the verses in *England's Helicon,* many poems by Barnfield, Breton and Barns, Peele's *Arraignment of Paris,* many of Greene's prose Romances, Drayton's *Shepherd's Garland* and *Shepherd's Sirena*, much of the verse and prose of Lodge, the pastorals of William Browne, Phineas Fletcher's *Sicelides* and *Piscatory Eclogues* and such a masterpiece in its kind as Day's *Parliament of Bees*. Whatever emotional value there may be in this poetry is intimated rather than expressed. No poetic afflatus mars the conscious artifice of design. The sophisticated children of the English Renaissance cultivated pastoral verse to celebrate their deliverance from the bucolic life. Of the exuberant and sophisticated elements in Elizabethan thought the latter finds clearest expression in Decorative verse. Lest it might be inferred from the titles and authors just mentioned that pastoral and Decorative verse are to be identified, a few pastorals not in the Decorative manner may be recalled. *Hymen's Triumph* by Daniel is too rich in sentiment to be Decorative verse. Fletcher's *Faithful Shepherdess* is too delicately sensuous and too powerfully imaginative. Jonson's *Sad Shepherd* has too little artificiality to meet the requirements of the genre. Finally *Lycidas* and *November* in *The Shepherd's Calendar,* both pastoral elegies, are treasuries not of Decorative but of the highest Intensive imagery, far transcending the type of Decorative poetry. With the latter type of poetry in mind, its typical imagery and more especially its use of the Decorative metaphor may be sketched.

Apart from a few of the most conventional metaphors the sum of the images in this poetry is not large. This is in part caused by the airy thinness to which ingenuity and perseverance frequently beat out a single figure. Campion makes of a single image the entire poem, "Follow thy fair sun, unhappy shadow." Two thirds of the sonnets in Drayton's *Idea's Mirror* show this technique. Sidney in *Astrophel and Stella,* Spenser in the *Amoretti,* and that scholar-poet, Drummond of Hawthornden, use it fre-

quently. Fewer Decorative figures, and notably fewer
Decorative figures of the extended type, appear in the se-
quences of Daniel and Shakespere. It is of course one of
the distinctions of Shakespere's greater sonnets that in
them the poignant Renaissance conception of love and time
is expressed for the most part not in the delicate flower
emblems of Ronsard, Spenser and Herrick, but in imagery
of truly sublime proportions. "When I have seen by
Time's fell hand defaced. . . ." The actual number of images in Shakespere's earlier plays is less than in his later
plays. A seemingly general impression that figures are
more abundant in the earlier plays, which incline more to
the Decorative type of poetry, is largely due to the ingenious torturing of single figures through several lines. A
conspicuous instance occurs in *Richard Second* where an
image of the state as a garden is the nucleus of an entire
scene (III, 4). By this device Richard's Queen learns
more gently than by a formal message the story of her
husband's dethronement.

Not all Decorative imagery is, as we have seen, contained
in Decorative verse, nor does all the imagery of Decorative
verse belong to that category. If the latter were the case
monotony would be the result. In *The Shepherd's Calendar* the political, the Decorative and the highly imaginative
eclogues are well distinguished, while imagery in each poem
is adapted to one of the three types of poetry and modified
in a manner which produces a harmony through the entire
sequence. It is the nature of Decorative imagery in light
verse to lead to the brink of higher forms of metaphorical
imagination and to fall short of them. A large part of the
art of Decorative verse is to keep the degree of the poet's
earnestness in suspense. Such a dangling with emotion is
to be seen in that consummate bit of sophisticated imagery
by Thomas Lodge, "*Love in my bosom like a bee.*" Many
poems in which Decorative imagery is involved show a

confusion in the types of metaphor. Greene's poem *"Like to Diana on her summer weed"* is in two stanzas. The first is in gorgeous Expansive imagery. The second illustrates throughout the Decorative form. In the *Shepherd's Garland,* an early pastoral series of Drayton's in imitation of Spenser, appears a still more marked confusion of types. Diggen Davie and Colin Clout go far deeper into devotional themes than their station in life would suggest, while a Decorative, pastoral imagery is rather inconsistently kept in view. That Drayton felt the incongruity and no doubt enjoyed it is witnessed in the following lines:

> Stay thou good Rowland, whither art thou rapt
> Beyond the moon that striveth thus to strain;
> Into what phrenzy lately art thou hapt?
> That in this sort intoxicates thy brain,
> Much disagreeing from a shepherd's strain.

V

The pastoral poets frequently enter the high chancel of poetic ritual in the guise of mischievous choir boys. No reader and perhaps not even the poets themselves could explain in precisely what spirit this verse is written. In subject, form and allusion the Decorative poetry of the Renaissance in England is largely classical; in its evasive temperament it shows a marked gothic inheritance. A survey of Decorative poetry, then, shows it to contain fewer figures beyond the inevitable conventions than might at first be supposed; it affects the tortured image; and just as it toys with incongruous sentiments, it toys with a confusion of metaphorical forms.

The relatively low plane of imagination in Decorative poetry is indicated by the prevalence of exemplification. Except for an occasional ingenuity of allusion this sober figure is the antithesis of the Decorative form. This is another of the paradoxes of Decorative verse. Side by side with the far-fetched but conventional conceits, which make the most imaginative adventures and bring back nothing better than pyrites, stand numerous exemplifications, figures below the level of metaphor itself. These figures are from one standpoint reduplications and redundancies. Typical of this copious and expanded style are the following lines from the *Prothalamion,* perhaps most beautiful of all Decorative poems:

> . . . That like old Peneus waters they do seem
> When down along by Tempe's pleasant shore,
> Scattered with flowers, through Thessaly they stream,
> That they appear, through lilies' plenteous store,
> Like a bride's chamber floor.

From one stream to another and from a flower-strewn stream to a flower-strewn chamber are no great leaps in imagination. In contrast with the mild manner of exemplification in the decorative *Prothalamion* may be noted the occasional honey-stinging Intensive metaphors in the *Epithalamion,* the companion poem conceived with so much greater enthusiasm:

> And harken to the bird's love-learned song
> The dewy leaves among.

The imaginative value of the Decorative image is not only depreciated from its internal structure, but by mass effect and a protracted accent upon the minor term is reduced still further. One of the most striking features of Decorative poetry is the massing of figures. An isolated metaphor is often too bare or of too brief endurance to have an assured value. By massing figures that may even have an appreciable imaginative value Decorative verse depreciates each and the sum of all. Sympathetic images become Decorative in the press. This technique is a favorite trick of Euphuism. The stanza from Campion in praise of the lily, rose and damask hue is sufficient to recall much longer passages. The general question of the interrelation

of metaphors will receive only slight attention in this
study.   Why one series accumulates the imaginative values
of the images while another depreciates them is by no
means obvious.   These lines from Marlowe's *Hero and
Leander* contain a metaphorical series of accumulative
power.

> A stately builded ship, well rigged and tall,
> The ocean maketh more majestical;
> Why vowest thou then to live in Sestos here,
> Who on love's seas more glorious wouldst appear?
> Like untuned golden strings all women are,
> Which long time lie untouched, will harshly jar;
> Vessels of brass oft handled brightly shine;
> What difference betwixt the richest mine
> And basest mold but use?   For both not used
> Are of like worth.   Then treasure is abused
> When misers keep it.   Being put to loan
> In time it will return us two to one.
> Rich robes themselves and others do adorn;
> Neither themselves nor others if not worn.
> Who builds a palace and shuts up the gate
> Shall see it ruinous and desolate.
> Ah, simple Hero, learn thyself to cherish!

Such images, which are largely of the Expansive category,
may be thought to have an almost intoxicating effect.   Emphasis accumulates from line to line.   Mass figures in Lyly
on the contrary grow less and less seriously affecting.   We
laugh at them much as we laugh at a similar technique in
Gilbert and Sullivan's farcical lyrics.   We flatter ourselves
for detecting an attempt to hide the insignificance of each
figure under the mass.   This metaphorical pita-patter is
agreeable enough—until it grows tiresome.   With mass
technique may be contrasted the equally striking technique
of rhetorical accent, carefully avoided in Decorative verse.
Such accent may be most clearly observed in a figure which
is transformed by it in part from the Decorative to the In-

tensive category. The generalization by which the Decorative metaphor of the lip and the rose-bud may be changed into the powerful Exuberant figure of love as "a red, red rose" has already been noted. Even in the hey-day of the rose convention, however, that image partly through expansion and partly by means of rhetorical accent appears in Shakespere with deep imaginative effect. This is especially instanced in one of those sonnets belonging, with numbers 30, 49, 57, 61, 71, 87, 90, 110, 111 and 119, to that group of intimate poems in which imagery is never elaborate or intrusive and sincerity almost at a whisper. The last line of the Hundred and Ninth Sonnet frames one figurative word in a parenthesis of accent. The entire structure of the poem hangs upon it. One of the most conventional images in poetry is adorned by splendid rhetoric alone. To a direct and exuberant enthusiasm like that of Burns Shakespere brings art. Rhetorically the poem is as though the eye should start from the left on the setting of a ring, circle it, and return to the gem. The technique of mass effect and isolation is clearly the reverse of the manner of Decorative verse, which casts roses with profusion and cheapens the price of all. One more observation on the spontaneous technique of the grouping of images should not be omitted. Exalted passages of involved and passionate imagery are in English poetry often edged with lines of extreme and literal simplicity, like masses of thundercloud bordered with calm moonlight. So in the Third Act of *King Lear:*

> Ye sulphurous and thought-executing fires,
> Vaunt-couriers of oak-cleaving thunder-bolts,
> Singe my white head . . .
> Come on, my boy. How dos't, my boy? Ar't cold?
> I am cold myself.
>
> III, 2, 4

One of the chief glories of the English poets is the incomparable imaginative range of their instrument.—But leaving the problems of the rhetoric of metaphor only hinted at, we must return to our analysis of the individual figure.

Misaccent is a still more general characteristic of Decorative poetry than profusion, and indeed underlies the definition of Decorative imagery itself. The imagist in light verse is often less interested in his nominal subject than in his metaphorical digression. Ingenuity is the life and breath of his poetry. Nothing shows ingenuity better than far-fetched metaphor. Consequently he views his Decorative images with particular favor. That Elizabethan sonnet writing represented more an art of metaphor than the art of love was throughout the period a notorious accusation. Sidney, Shakespere and Drayton are in their sonnet collections their own apologists. Misaccent is a matter of interpretation. Impressions are difficult to justify. The misaccented images of William Browne are however fortunately conclusive in themselves. The metaphors of this poet are to say the least novel. The *Fifth Song* in the First Book of *Britannia's Pastorals* may be regarded as his masterpiece. Still clinging to the Decorative pastoral tradition he introduces by way of metaphor in this poem observations on the life of his own beloved country-side. The explanation is not difficult. There was in Browne's day little opportunity for pictures of everyday rural life in polite verse. Browne compromised by introducing them in simile. Nine similes comprise more than a fifth of the entire number of lines in his Song. Their topics are as follows:

Children playing on the beach............. 1–12
Children on their way from school......... 63–70
A swan 129–141
A ship on the north seas.................. 441–458
A country blacksmith..................... 501–516
A girl practicing at the virginals.......... 621–634

The sixth figure is typical.

> As when a maid taught from her mother wing
> To tune her voice unto a silver string,
> When she should run she rests, rests when should run,
> And ends her lesson now it is begun.
> Now misseth she her stop, then in her song,
> And doing of her best she still is wrong.
> Begins again, and yet again strikes false,
> Then in a chafe forsakes her virginals;
> And yet within an hour she tries anew;
> That with her daily pains, art's chiefest due,
> She gains that charming skill, and can no less
> Tame the fierce tigers in the wilderness
> Than that Oengrin harpist for whose lay
> Tigers with hunger pined and left their prey;
> So Riot, when he gan to climb the hill,
> Here maketh haste and there long standeth still.

The Decorative depreciation lies in what is here the relative insignificance of Riot and the charming picture of a girl at her music lesson. The Decorative ingenuity of the figure, which Lyly's platitudes in platitudinous metaphor so frequently lack, lies in the utterly far-fetched comparison. What could be more unlike the pretty impatience of the novice in playing madrigals than the idea of Riot panting and storming a hill? Yet we are indebted to this freakishness of Browne's for bits of rustic realism that at times suggest John Clare; and in the image in lines 807–832 may be found the probable germ of Keat's *Eve of Saint Agnes*. An image representative of Browne's intimate love of nature may be taken from the Second Song:

> Like to that smell which oft our sense descries
> Within a field which long unploughed lies,

Somewhat before the setting of the sun,
And where the rainbow on the horizon
Doth pitch his tips.

333

The fragrance of summer grass after a shower seems to
have attracted Browne more than his artificial shepherds.
His metaphors are generously incongruous. They constitute one of the most fantastic turns in the story of Elizabethan imagery.

The history of the introduction of Decorative metaphor
into Tudor poetry is in itself a generous subject of research.
Passing over the history of the form on the Continent and
the story of its adaptation by the sixteenth century Englishmen, along with innumerable other Continental fashions,
we find the form well established in the poetry of Wyatt
and Surrey. The greater artificiality and sophistication
of Wyatt's verses, especially those imitated from Serafino,
make them much richer in Decorative metaphor than the
sweetly sentimental, highly personal and ingenuous lyrical
effusions which make the younger poet beloved. In their
translations from Petrarch and in all that is owed to common sources they are much alike. The genius of Wyatt
was largely for Decorative verse, that of Surrey for idylic
verse. Yet when Wyatt is thoroughly in earnest his poetry
tends to a straightforward literal style. In two of his best
known poems for example, *"And wilt thou leave me thus"*
and *"Forget not yet the tried intent,"* not a single image
occurs. Thus a distinction between the metaphorical
manner in serious and Decorative verse was early established. Googe, Turberville, Churchyard, Gascoigne and
the contributors to the earlier anthologies show little originality in Decorative figures, but conscientiously employ a
limited number of conventional conceits. Thomas Watson,
with his extensive borrowings from abroad, marks a considerable advance. Not until the verse of Lyly, Spenser,

Drayton, Greene and Lodge, however, does the ruthless tiger that adorned the pastoral world of Surrey and Turberville find more terrible enemies than himself to fear or more dreadful objects than of old to look upon. The grim medieval grotesques of horror became the spleenful unicorns and painted dragons which delighted the Renaissance. The chief event in the development of Decorative imagery is the new subtlety of the figures in *The Shepherd's Calendar.* The new type definitely replaced the wooden and amusingly awkward images of the mid-century poets. Spenser and Harvey in their correspondence praise metaphors which are not only far-fetched in learning, as those of Lyly, but far-fetched in imaginative ingenuity. A mechanical imitation of Continental forms gives way to lively if not exalted artistic creation.

Two figures from Greene may be taken to show how far in advance of the stock images of Wyatt's verse inventive ingenuity had developed, and how far the poetic imagination had still to go to liberate itself from what one critic, Samuel L. Wolff, has well called "the jingle and glitter of chains."

Parrhasius drawing the counterfeit of love painted him tickling Youth on the left side with a feather and stinging him on the right with a scorpion.

Perimides, p. 70

Phidias the painter drew . . . Mars tied unto Venus by the eye, his breast open, wherein appeared a heart all of gold. But Venus having her sight veiled, her heart pierced through with an arrow and chained unto Mars with a silver thread, wherein was written this poesy, " *Sans Aultre.*"

Tritameron, p. 75

George Chapman half mockingly voices the spirit of this new poetry thus:

> Your wit is of the true Pierian spring
> That can make anything of anything.

It would be rash to say that in all cases the Elizabethan conceitists were trifling with love. The analogy of controversial writing would indicate otherwise. John Penry and many controversialists of both parties gladly offered their lives in martyrdom for beliefs which they defended in jesting pamphlets. We must be prepared for many such seeming inconsistencies in the Renaissance mind. What then does this elaborate imaginative manner signify in Elizabethan thought? The modern reader is in danger of being fooled by his own industry. It is not agreeable to contemplate that an image which one thinks was written in pain was a joke, or that a figure which one thinks was written in jest was written in earnest. This is quite possible in reading such deceptive and sophisticated poetry. To reduce this probability and to come into closer sympathy with an elusive form is the chief purpose of this chapter.

The courtly fashion of fantastic imagery owed its principal stimulus to the ''ink-horn'' of Lyly. This fashion may best be thought of as a game. In an imaginative age which gave to the fancy fewer toys indoors than our own, the most convenient game for the courtiers was a match of tongues. This sport resembled a game not only in gaiety, contention and inconsequence, but in the readiness with which it was laid aside. Euphuism was all of life on the comic stage alone. A little salt of realism in comedy itself shows the convention transient and modish. Benedick and Beatrice quickly come to a situation that makes clever imagery impertinent. In the crucial scenes appear such stripped and cutting phrases as ''Kill Claudio.'' To imagine that the courtiers always spoke in the conceited style would be equivalent to thinking that Johnson always spoke in Johnsonese. Lyly's language to a butcher cannot have been elaborated with the imagery that won applause from lords and ladies. Business of a pressing character dispensed with Euphuism, as the correspondence of the period amply shows. "Our men were hardy," says Drayton, and though hardy men may play with Euphuism their language in action will be rough, literal and hard. The Elizabethans were Spartans in the field and on the sea, Euphuists in courteous parley and at the court. The narratives in Hakluyt are bare, the language of the tavern fantastic. When an Elizabethan captain put off his cloak of ceremony and donned his sea cloak he largely dispensed with his decorated language. How closely the dance of images that prevailed at Elizabeth's court reflected the manners and temperament of a giddy age may be understood from a study of sixteenth century architecture, costume and Decorative art, and from the social literature of the period. Elizabethan taste was shocked by an undecorated wall. Two instances from the social literature will suffice here. Stubbes' *Anatomy of Abuses* tells of a barber shop which had recently been established after the Continental fashion. It is the symbol of the generation of Satan. On entering this shop the customer was saluted by music. He was next asked whether he was going to the wars or to court. If he were going to the wars he would want his hair cut "ferociously"; if he were going to court he would want it cut "voluptuously." On leaving he paid the barber as much as he chose. The national mind which conceived such a barber shop is illustrated by the metaphors cited in the preceding pages. Though I would not give undue stress to the fashions of Elizabethan hair cutting, another passage must be cited in evidence of the imaginative temper of the age.

How, sir, will you be trim'd? Will you have your beard like a spade or a bodkin? A penthouse on your upper lip or an alley on your chin? A low curl on your head like a bull or a dangling lock like a spaniel? Your mustacheos sharp at the ends like shoemakers' awls or hanging down to your mouth

like goats' flakes? Your love locks wreathed with a silken
twist or shaggy to fall on your shoulders?

Lyly, Midas, III, 1

Perhaps a still more suggestive illustration of the spirit of
this Decorative imagery may be found in the following
from Earle's Microcosmographie. Earle praises the ac-
complished cook.

> His cunning is not small in architecture, for he builds
> strange fabrics in paste, towers and castles, which are offered
> to the assault of valiant teeth, and like Darius his palace in
> one banquet demolished.

The Elizabethans not only spoke but behaved themselves
fantastically. A study of their metaphors helps to interpret their behavior. The preliminary facts regarding the
development and significance of their Decorative imagery
may, then, be summarized as follows: the form is well exemplified in Wyatt, wooden in his immediate successors,
and takes new life in Spenser and in the poetry that follows The Shepherd's Calendar; it is as much a feature of
conversation as of verse; it may be regarded as a game for
gallants and courtiers, neglected or assumed on fitting occasions; and finally it reflects the fantastic spirit of the
age, and the restless mind of the Renaissance itself.

The poets themselves can best resolve the ambiguity of
sentiment which characterizes the form. Gascoigne and
Spenser, as we have already seen, defend metaphorical ingenuity for its own sake, a position which Jonson resolutely
attacks. Innumerable passages throw light on this engaging psychological problem. "Many become passionate
lovers only to win praise of their wits," writes Nash in
Jack Wilton concerning Surrey's mythical adventures
with Geraldine.

Let us turn first to Shakespere. The bewildering com-
plexity of sentiment lurking in these fantastical figures is
illustrated in two passages of Love's Labor's Lost.

With that, they all did tumble on the ground,
With such a zelous laughter, so profound,
That in this spleen ridiculous appears,
To check their folly, passion's solemn tears.

V, 2, 115

Taffeta phrases, silken terms precise,
  Three-piled hyperboles, spruce affectation;
Figures pedantical; these summer flies
  Have blown me full maggot ostentation.

V, 2, 406

The second quatrain is an admirable commentary on the language and character of Holofernes, the high priest of the pedantical conceit. Decorative verse leading laughter on the left hand and passion on the right was queen over the children of the hour. Shakespere's Hundred and Thirtieth Sonnet, "My mistress' eyes are nothing like the sun," is an arraignment of the conceited style. No more valuable critique can be found than the character of Falconbridge. The second act of *King John* is a persistent but not altogether conclusive satire on conceited language. English and French armies frown upon each other terribly in Flanders, while kings, ambassadors and townspeople join in a war of horrible devices. The young Falconbridge, a sturdy patriotic and altogether typical Englishman, fights as effectively with his tongue in parley as with his arms in battle. He playfully observes that the French king has in metaphor drawn his mistress in his eye, quartered her in his heart and hung her on his brow. This is a typical passage:

Here's a large mouth indeed,
That spits forth death and mountains, rocks and seas,
Talks as familiarly of roaring lions
As maids of thirteen do of puppy dogs.
What cannoner begot this lusty blood?

> He speaks plain cannon fire, and smoke and bounce;
> He gives the bastinado with his tongue;
> Our ears are cudgell'd, not a word of his
> But buffets better than a fist of France.
> Zounds! I was never so bethump'd with words
> Since I first call'd my brother's father dad!

Falconbridge ridicules equally the Violent image or fustian and the Decorative image or the conceit. In a joyous exercise of unfettered ingenuity the conceitist laughs at his own excess. Throughout this scene the hero impudently repeats an absurd figure of a lion's heart in a calf's skin, quite as far-fetched as the language of the Frenchmen. Close upon this robust nonsense follow the celebrated images of the painted lily, the perfumed violet and the rainbow adorned. In the prison scene far-fetched metaphors ornament pathetic speeches. From the standpoint of imagery this play is a medley. The Elizabethans appear to have distinguished earnest and jest in metaphor with little consistency. Figures of the same imaginative value are viewed with ridicule or admiration. One moment the poets mock the elaborate language of court and the next realize that it answers a whimsical desire in their own nature.

Even in the moment of Benedick's challenge his ingenious and irrepressible metaphors are a cloak to hide his emotion. Claudio jests away his difficulty with Euphuism. After listening to the puns of the heroic John of Gaunt on his death bed, Richard II asks, "Can sick men play so nicely with their names?" To this Gaunt replies, "No, misery makes sport to mock itself." These episodes illustrate a common emotional state. As an offset to exuberance the Elizabethan whipped his fiery nature into bounds with the Senecan ideal of stoical repression. Proud men screened their suffering, and at the same time sharpened and embittered it, by Euphuistic language.

A ready way to distinguish conscious rhetoric from fancy

and the Decorative from the more sympathetic categories is to observe the change in the imagery of Romeo after he has seen Juliet. Before the meeting his figures are prevailingly Decorative and superficial. After that scene, in which he addresses Juliet in the ritualistic metaphors of Intensive imagery, his figures are chiefly Expansive and Exuberant. Decorative figures are here associated with a relatively slight and unstable passion.

The familiar theme of ingenuity that beguiles pain is dramatically exhibited in the dialogue between Desdemona and Iago on the shore of Cyprus. Iago's confession of the intellectual and essentially unimaginative character of his conceits is of exceptional interest.

DES. I am not merry; but I do beguile
      The thing I am, by seeming otherwise—
      Come, how wouldst thou praise me?
IAGO I am about it; but indeed my invention
      Comes from my pate as birdlime does from frieze;
      It plucks out brains and all. But my Muse labors
      And thus she is delivered. . . .
DES. These are old fond paradoxes to make fools laugh i'
      the alehouse.

                                 II, 1, 123

Mr. W. J. Graig, editor of the Alden edition of *The Merry Wives of Windsor,* says: "Perhaps the most unnatural bit of Falstaff in this play is the Kissing Comfit scene, as it is the climax. His images appear to me so truly absurd, so far-fetched and improbable, that it is monstrous to suppose they were conceived in anything but the severest spirit of irony." When Sir John was stirred no further than the bottom of Mistress Ford's pocket book he chose to quote, or intentionally to misquote, a line from Sir Philip Sidney. Whether Shakespere intended the character of Falstaff at this point to be a moral satire or not, he clearly showed that Sidney's love poetry lent itself to the lips of unromantic lovers. Equally certain is it that Shakespere did not mean "the severest irony" to extend to Sir Philip Sidney. The usual metaphorical protestations of affection were evidently expected and enjoyed, but in the personal sense valued for little. Romantic images were indeed sadly profaned. "As morning roses newly washed with dew!" shouts Petrucio, in high hopes of winning and taming Kate. To much the same effect are some lines in George Chapman's *All Fools*.

> " One that is rich enough, her hair pure amber,
> Her forehead mother of pearl, her fair eyes
> Two wealthy diamonds, her lips like rubies;
> Her teeth are orient pearl, her neck pure ivory."
> —Jest not, good sir, in an affair so serious.

All Fools, I, 253

Two lyrics powerfully summarize the poets' own criticism of Decorative imagery. The first is found at the close of one of the most consistently Decorative book of verses during the period, Campion's *Book of Airs*. It supplies exactly what the student seeks, an expression of the philosophy from which such poetry springs. These lines remind him to look beneath the dainty fooling of Elizabethan Decorative poetry with a probability of finding, like a scorpion under a stone, deep moral restlessness, skepticism and despair.

> Whether men do laugh or weep,
> Whether they do wake or sleep,
> Whether they die young or old,
> Whether they feel heat or cold,
> There is underneath the sun
> Nothing in true earnest done.
>
> All our pride is but a jest,
> None are worst and none are best,
> Grief and joy and hope and fear
> Play their pageants everywhere.

> Vain opinion all doth sway,
> And this world is but a play.
>
> Powers above in clouds do sit
> Mocking our poor apish wit,
> That so lamely with such state
> Their high glory imitate.
> No ill can be felt but pain,
> And that happy men disdain.

If a poem made up of an handful of Decorative images seem slight, cold, unworthy of great poetry or of studious reading we may recall that beneath it not improbably lies a sting. A part of the fascination of such verse lies in the mystery of what long dried up poison its delicate vessel may once have contained.

Even Drayton hid his honest heart under a cloak of metaphor. In one illuminating sonnet he gives away the secret. Because he is fully representative of his age and because no one has made a clearer confession, his poem is of unusual interest. Campion's lyric betrays the gall in Decorative verse. Drayton reconciles it with his own invulnerable honesty.

> I hear some say, " This man is not in love.
> Who can he love? A likely thing," they say.
> " Read but his verse and it will easily prove."—
> O judge not rashly, gentle sir, I pray,
> Because I loosely trifle in this sort
> As one that fain his sorrows would beguile.
> You now suppose me all this while in sport
> And please yourself with this conceit the while.
> You shallow censurers, sometime see you not
> In greatest perils some men pleasant be,
> Where fame by death is only to be got
> They resolute: so stands the case with me.
>   Where other men in depth of passion cry
>   I laugh at fortune, as in jest to die.

III

THE SUNKEN IMAGE

A Sunken image is one which powerfully affects the imagination without conveying a definite picture. It is to be distinguished from faded imagery. In the latter no definite picture is conveyed but neither is the imagination aroused. Thus the word platform, meaning a declaration of a political party, though potentially a metaphor is generally used without metaphorical intention. It is not a Sunken image. The category is equally distinguished from the fantastic incongruities of Decorative imagery and from the more elaborate and fully developed forms of poetic metaphor. The restraint of the figure commends it to writers of the classical school. Citing a Sunken image from Corneille, Voltaire writes that happy use of such figurative expression bequeaths the work of a poet to posterity. In *Cinna* the Emperor Augustus wearies of his great attainment. "Et monté sur le faîte, il aspire à descendre." Voltaire's comment is as follows:

Racine admirait surtout ce vers, et le faisait admirer par ses enfants. (Voy. les *Mem. de L. Racine*) En effet ce mot aspire, qui d'ordinaire s'emploie avec s'élever, devient une beauté frappante quand on le joint à descendre; c'est cet heureux emploi des mots, qui fait la belle poésie, et qui fait passer un ouvrage à la postérité.

The classical poet may conceal a use of metaphor, but he cannot dispense with it. No speech of emotional value can dispense with imagery. There is at least one form of imagery which appears both in the poetry of Shakespere and in the poetry of Corneille, Racine and Voltaire. An examination of the Sunken figures in Elizabethan literature affords a liberalizing view of the period.

A surprising number of Shakespere's most memorable lines are cast into the mold of Sunken metaphor. The larger part of the present section therefore will be devoted to a study of his peculiar cultivation of the more elusive form. Among his fellow poets Daniel ranks here the highest. Though Daniel is by no means severe, he is seldom bold. The sobriety of his metaphor marks him as a precursor of Dryden. Observing first some highly obscure metaphors of Shakespere and gradually passing to his more tangible figures the general tendencies of this category will rapidly unfold themselves.

The first image cited in the Introduction may serve as a type here.

EDGAR Men must endure
    Their going hence, even as their coming hither;
    Ripeness is all. Come on.
GLOS.   And that's true too.
            V, 2, 9

Upon the metaphor in these lines falls not an inconsiderable part of the intellectual burden of the tragedy. It is the oracular metaphor that philosophy receives from poetry. No definite image is aroused. No attempt to elaborate the figure is profitable. To fancy that its meaning is that the much experienced man finds life more significant in the fruit than in the flower, or that the chief wisdom of life is a recognition of the inevitable, or the seasonable, only detracts from the moral dignity of the utterance, for the image includes all these meanings and much beside. Both terms of the figures are cryptic. In such an extreme vagueness Sunken imagery may be seen arising from obscurity.

Several causes keep poetic metaphor below full visibility. An insufficient hint may be given from which the im-

age is to be aroused. Such is the case in the phrase from
King Lear. A violent incongruity may render it unpleas-
ing to image two figures completely, but pleasurable to associate their parts. A word may contain alternative images with the result that one picture blurs another present
on the same film. An agreeable stimulus may be had from
carrying a metaphor half way to completion when to realize it fully would be incongruous. Some images comprehend too much for full visualization and approach but do
not attain abstraction. All these cases illustrate the definition of the category. Definition must precede interpretation, which concerns the presence of the type in elevated,
serious and reflective passages, its strength, its poignancy
and its vigor.

Here is another figure representative of those in which
no sufficient hint for complete visualization is given.

> Then true Pisanio,—
> Who long'st, like me, to see thy lord; who long'st, . . .
> But in a fainter kind;—O not like me,
> For mine's beyond beyond!
>
> *Cym.* III, 2, 54

The imagination has no clue to fasten upon. The whole
passage from which these lines are taken is in a pure elusive metaphor which only Imogen, Rosalind, Juliet and the
elect of Shakespere's heroines have spoken. The distinction between such an ecstatic phrase as "beyond beyond"
and such an intellectually refined image as that cited from
Corneille is more easily made by taste than analysis. One
may recognize a certain geometric simplicity in Corneille's
figure, but then no briefer definition of infinity can be
found than the words of Imogen. So far as a definition of
imagery goes the two forms must be regarded as identical,
although no two figures could arise from more divergent
causes. The distinction is one of interpretation.

To appreciate the emphasis thrown upon the word "shock" in the following passage it is necessary to receive the full impetus of the poet's rhetoric. These are, save one, the closing lines of *King John.*

> This England never did nor ever shall
> Lie at the proud foot of a conqueror,
> But when it first did help to wound itself.
> Now these her princes are come home again,
> Come the three corners of the world in arms
> And we shall shock them.
>
> V, 7, 112

The student of metaphor inquires: 'how shock'? As a vessel is sunk on a reef, as a charger is staggered by a blow, or as a wave breaks against a headland? None of these comes precisely to mind and yet the word accumulates the force of all. Such language, in Voltaire's words, makes poetry for posterity.

The dialogue between Brutus and Cassius is brought to a conclusion with these words:

> The deep of night has crept upon our talk,
> And nature must obey necessity.
>
> *Caesar,* IV, 3, 226

"The deep of night" is a metaphor but an impenetrable one. That it should creep upon the dialogue of the reconciled patriots makes it more mysterious still. The sum of all creeping things is metaphorically associated with impenetrable darkness.

These lines are addressed by Duncan to Macbeth:

> Thou art so far before,
> The swiftest wing of recompense is slow
> To overtake thee.
>
> I, 4, 16

Several figurative suggestions occur here, but all subside into the passing of a wing of recompense, heard but not seen.

Many subdued images are to be found in the exuberant passages of the Histories. These are typical.

> Therein should we read
> The very bottom of the soul of hope.
>
> *I Hen. IV,* IV, 1, 49

> The winter lion, who in rage forgets
> Aged contusions and all brush of time
> And, like a gallant in the brow of youth,
> Repairs him with occasion.
>
> *II Hen. VI,* V, 3, 2

The second passage suggests the figurative manner of Marlowe. "Brush" calls up a host of delicate and vanishing images. "Brow" shows a much fuller visualization. The figurative conception of the forehead may seem too violent for complete realization but agreeable when partly realized. Shakespere uses the image variously, sometimes hinting at a severe and sometimes at an open beauty.

> Why here walk I in the black brow of night.
>
> *John,* V, 6, 17

> As Philomel in summer's front doth sing
> And stops her pipe in growth of riper days.
>
> *Son.* 102

The metaphor from *King John* violently spurns a thoroughgoing visualization. To walk in the black brow of night is no sober possibility. The figure is impressionistic. It prepares the mind for the story of the treacherous poisoning of the King. The five succeeding citations further illustrate the impossibility of full realization because of a confusion of ideas.

> O how shall summer's honey breath hold out
> Against the wreckful siege of battering days.
>
> *Son.* 65

O here
Will I set up my everlasting rest
And shake the yoke of inauspicious stars
From this world-wearied flesh.

Rom. and Jul. V, 3, 109

There is no sure foundation set on blood.

John, IV, 2, 104

Yet be sad good brothers;
For, by my faith, it very well becomes you.
Sorrow so royally in you appears
That I will deeply put the fashion on
And wear it in my heart.

II Hen. IV, V, 2, 49

There is a history in all mens' lives,
Figuring the nature of the time's deceas'd
The which observed, a man may prophesy
With a near aim, of the main chance of things
As yet not come to life, who in their seeds
And weak beginnings lie intreasured.

Ib. III, 1, 80

A literal-minded reader might take such figures as these
for more than seems intended. As great a sensitiveness
appears in declining the incongruous suggestions of metaphor as in accepting its pertinent ones. These figures are
not the monstrosities of mixed metaphor which a matter of
fact interpretation declares them. No wreckful battery
and siege could find a foothold on so disembodied a substance as honnied breath. Fully conceived the figure is
manifestly absurd, yet most readers will find it exquisitely
beautiful. The citations from *Romeo and Juliet* and *King
John* are memorable lines in a metaphorical manner which
belongs to the poet's earlier style. Without decreasing in
vigor and boldness, his later imagery shows a gain in subtlety. The fourth figure is dignified but strongly sympathetic. Although a formality that befits the language of

the newly crowned King appropriately restrains imagination, the lines are rich in poetic suggestion. They convey at once a comeliness and a sincerity of sorrow. Sunken imagery is the most felicitous for the occasion. The last citation shows the form on the familiar ground of reflective poetry. It suggests the kinship of Shakespere and Bacon, who lend to reflection an abundant power of metaphorical imagination.

Many Sunken images in Shakespere approach but do not realize personification. A prevalence of merely perfunctory personifications is one of the marks of an unimaginative age. This convention in much eighteenth century verse fails to stir the pictorial imagination from its lethargy. Capitalization more strongly affects the appearance of the page than the personified figures print themselves on the mind. Shakespere hints at a figure in personification without an insistence on a nondescript human form, and directs attention to some emblem or attribute which gives vivid existence to the abstract idea. Sometimes his poetry strikes life into an inanimate object which may be thought to attach itself to a personified figure. Because these personifications are rather intimated than expressed they are associated with Sunken imagery. Most of the eighteenth century personifications have on the contrary no metaphorical elements whatsoever. A passage from *Antony and Cleopatra* illustrates the Shakesperian technique.

> Upon your sword
> Sit laurel victory, and smooth success
> Be strew'd before your feet!

> I, 3, 99

A personified idea cannot be strewed. Victory and success are clearly intended as parallel ideas. It is awkward to imagine victory a goddess and success a carpet covered with flowers. Hence victory is not personified. The epithet "laurel" makes it difficult to think of victory as a

bird of Jove seated upon the sword. Victory is nothing
more than a naked, cutting and triumphant weapon. The
hand of Anthony animates it with far more spirit than belongs to the painted abstractions of an obsolete mythology.
In the choice between metaphor and bare personification
Shakespere as the poet of the modern world gave preference to metaphor. These citations may be added to that
from *Antony and Cleopatra.*

> But look, amazement on thy mother sits!
> O step between her and her fighting soul.
>> *Ham.* III, 4, 112

> Vengence ride upon our swords.
>> *T. and C.,* V, 3, 47

> Let me sit heavy on thy soul to-morrow.
>> *Rich. III,* V, 3, 118

> Gainst death and all oblivious enmity
> Shall you pace forth.
>> *Son.* 55

> I hope not dead.
>> He's walk'd the way of nature;
> And to our purposes he lives no more.
>> *II Hen. IV,* V, 2, 4

A final example of Shakespere's genius for symbolizing abstractions with only intimated personifications occurs in
the description of Romeo's apothecary.

> Contempt and beggary hangs upon thy back;
> The world is not thy friend nor the world's law.
>> V, 1, 71

It is impossible to think of two classical abstractions in human form attacking the impoverished apothecary from behind. The verb it will be observed is singular. Like
Wordsworth's leach-gatherer, a figure from vulgar life becomes an embodiment of general ideas. The poet has at

once struck life into the apothecary's rags and life into two of our most powerful abstractions. This is thoroughly in the Shakesperian manner. The universality which the eighteenth century poets so often sought ineffectually by conventional personification he triumphantly attains.

The Elizabethans frequently formalized their style by reference not to remote and Olympian themes but to the commonplace and familiar. This practice illustrates the robust character of their thought and the elaborate-mindedness already discussed under the head of the Decorative image as motivated by Renaissance culture. These realistic figures are often protracted and so hardy that only an incomplete realization makes them palatable. Although artificially elaborated they are more than Decorative trifles. They belong accordingly to the category of the Sunken image. The opening of The Seventy-Fourth Sonnet has been praised especially for moral calm and poetic dignity. It exemplifies this type of imagery.

> But be contented! When the fell arrest
> Without all bail shall carry me away
> My life hath in this line some interest
> Which for memorial still with thee shall stay.

One would either not find such imagery in modern verse or find it in humorous verse. A bailiff would have seemed misplaced in serious verse of the Victorian poets. To Shakespere, Greene, Nash, Dekker, Heywood and the larger number of their contemporaries poetry has no distinction between the matter of fact and the world of fancy. They were associated on as impartial terms as the Matter of Troy and the Matter of Charlemagne in the Romances. Whatever was touched by the imagination of a true poet was deemed gold. Poetry was not an abstraction from the mass of experience but the vision which transformed the mass. Beauty sprang up in dusty corners. If the poet were true to his inspiration no object for metaphor could be incongruent or coarse. He could no more soil his hands with a vulgar figure than a gentleman could be debased by manual labor in a time of necessity. This is the view of life and art which colors the imagery of The Seventy-Fourth Sonnet. Recognizing the principle one may still think the metaphor strained. It is difficult however to dislike the daring catholic idealism which emanating from Elizabethan poetry has charmed, soothed and inspired many generations and done more than any single feature to make that poetry cherished, prized and beloved. There will be more to say of this in succeeding chapters.

Sunken images which call up two or more conflicting pictures destroying a clear metaphorical conception have been compared to the blur of two or more pictures on the same film of a camera. The following may serve as an illustration.

> Whilst bloody treason flourisht over us.
> *Caesar,* III, 2, 196

The figure may with equal propriety be thought to refer to trees, banners, trumpets, swords and perhaps much more.

Dismissing figures of interest from the standpoint of definition the question remains how often and with what significance the form appears. Computation on this subject would be inaccurate and futile. Sunken metaphor is a staple of Elizabethan poets both in exuberant and sober verse, and is almost as frequently used in the prose of Bacon and Nash as in the poetry of Spenser and Shakespere. Though it is not Shakespere's greatest type of metaphor it is perhaps his greatest distinction in metaphor. His genius is well known to be for the concrete word. In these two lines for example five of the six major words have figurative ore and four of the five suggest new veins of imagery.

> That can translate the stubborness of fortune
> Into so quiet and so sweet a style.
>
> *A. Y. L. I.* II, 1, 19

One becomes so accustomed to figurative language in Shakespere as to imagine it at times where it is not. These familiar lines from *As You Like It* for instance might at a glance be thought Sunken imagery:

> Your virtues, gentle master,
> Are sanctified and holy traitors to you.
>
> II, 3, 13

This is pure analogy, not metaphor. Because the thought of Adam is so profoundly imaginative the impression is akin to imagery. In fact nothing could be less figurative. It is the simple transparency of truth.

Sunken metaphor opens the imagination to a greater range of receptivity, arouses fear or expectation, gives poignancy, vigor and power, and is especially effective in noble, elevated or contemplative passages. All these characteristics may best be illustrated from Shakespere. The following figures are selected to illustrate a tendency to open the imagination to a greater range of receptivity. Although far removed from the Expansive category, they are a growth of the same soil. In each case visualization even for Sunken imagery is exceptionally vague.

> What lady's that, which doth enrich the hand
> Of yonder knight?
>
> *Rom. and Jul.* I, 5, 42

> Rich music's tongue.
>
> *Rom. and Jul.* II, 6, 27

> Thou dearest Perdita,
> With these forc'd thoughts, I prithee, darken not
> The mirth o' the feast.
>
> *W. T.* IV, 4, 40

Under the shade of melancholy boughs
Lose and neglect and the creeping hours of time.

A. Y. L. I. II, 7, 111

So that eternal love in love's fresh case
Weighs not the dust and injury of age.

Son. 108

O this false soul of Egypt . . .
Like a right gipsy, hath, at fast and loose,
Beguil'd me to the very heart of lose.

Ant. and Cleo. IV, 12, 25

The lady and music are the sum of all that is rich and precious. What manner of darkness threatens Perdita's mirth is impressively left untold. This darkness is rather felt than seen. For the subtle imagery in the citation from *As You Like It* each reader will have a personal explanation. In the line from the Sonnets the metaphor is that of a traveller covered with the dust of the road, who has sustained some rude bruises from his journey. So much may fairly be assumed. What manner of injuries he has sustained, however, each reader must imagine for himself. "To the very heart of lose" is the metaphor of Antony's utmost tragic despair. These five figures stimulate the imagination without satisfying it. They are at the lowest mark of visibility. Paradoxically they might be called disembodied imagery.

The Sunken metaphor comes readily to one who does not dare to express his hope or fear or who finds himself in some respect mystified. Obscure images of terror are especially notable in the Shakesperian tragedy. In the following subdued figures, ideas of dread and mystery find a tongue.

the Queen,
The sweet'st, dear'st creature's dead, and vengence for't
Not dropp'd down yet!

W. T. III, 2, 201

On horror's head horrors accumulate.

> *Oth.* III, 3, 370

>   our little life
> Is rounded with a sleep.

> *Tem.* IV, 1, 158

> You are too shallow, Hastings, much too shallow
> To sound the bottom of the after-times.

> *II Hen. IV,* 2, 50

One feels the incompleteness of these figures. With the aid of another word the metaphorical term, it seems, might be made clear; but that word terror or necessity forbids. The questions how vengeance will drop from heaven and in what sense life is surrounded by a mysterious slumber remain unanswered. No fully rounded metaphor could so well express the nameless horror of Othello or the inability of Hastings to unriddle the secrets of futurity.

Shakespere at times gives zest to an abstract idea by a surprisingly vigorous, naturalistic and concrete metaphor. The violent contrast between abstract and concrete discourages complete visualization. These figures give a tonic quality to the poet's thought.

>   it is great
> To do that thing that ends all other deeds;
> Which shackles accidents and bolts up change;

> *Ant. and Cleo.* V, 2, 4

>   now all labor
> Mars what it does; yea, very force entangles
> Itself with strength.

> *Ant. and Cleo.* IV, 14, 47

> There's a divinity that shapes our ends
> Rough-hew them how we will.

> *Ham.* V, 2, 10

        Is this the nature
Whom passions could not shake? whose solid virtue
The shot of accident nor dart of chance
Could neither graze nor pierce?
Oth. IV, 1, 276

They say best men are molded out of faults.
M. for M. V, 1, 444

These citations are taken from emphatic passages. With
the language of Sunken metaphor Antony and Cleopatra
meet their destinies, one in sorrow and the other in pride.
In the same language Hamlet sums up his adventures,
Lodovico comments on the misfortunes of Othello, and
Mariana expresses an idea on which a large part of *Measure for Measure* depends. The consequence of figurative
language in these reflective passages is power.

Another consequence of subdued metaphor is poignancy.
This figure is found more often than Exuberant forms in
bitter, piercing scenes of sympathy or distress. Suffering
that is too confused to find collected expression in the symbol of ritual or too far numbed to precipitate itself in
vigorous imagination finds such utterance as this:

Cans't thou not minister to a mind diseas'd,
Pluck from the memory a rooted sorrow,
Raze out the written troubles of the brain,
And with some sweet oblivious antidote
Cleanse the stuff'd bosom of that perilous stuff
Which weighs upon the heart?
Mac. V, 3, 40

There's a great spirit gone . . .
The hand could pluck her back that shov'd her on.
Ant. and Cleo. I, 2, 126

O my dear father! Restoration hang
Thy medicine on my lips; and let this kiss
Repair those violent harms that my two sisters
Have in thy reverence made.
Lear, IV, 7, 26

What means this?
'Tis one of those odd tricks which sorrow shoots
Out of the mind.

Ant. and Cleo. IV, 2, 13

If she had partaken of my flesh, and caused me the dearest groans of a mother, I could not have owed her a more rooted love.

All's Well, IV, 5, 11

Surprise me to the very brink of tears.

Tim. V, 1, 159

I am sorry that such sorrow I procure;
And so deep sticks it in my penitent heart
That I crave death more willingly than mercy.

M. for M. V, 1, 479

How sharp the point of this remembrance is.—
My dear son Ferdinand!

Tem. V, 1, 138

He wrings at some distress.
Would I could free't!

Cym. III, 7, 79

Macbeth's subdued images expressive of his tenderness for the Queen follow and precede Expansive figures in the same scene. When Antony hears of the death of his wife his metaphorical afflatus deserts him. He speaks in the simplest imagery. The same faint thread of metaphor runs through Cordelia's greeting to her mad father. In the same language the faithful Enobarbus comments on Antony's fit of sadness. The unhappy Countess in *All's Well That Ends Well* only gives a figurative hint of her deep and unutterable regret for Helena. The heroic Coriolanus discloses in only the most reserved speech his unwonted tenderness. The imagery of Angelo and Alonso is all but silenced by the sting of shame; and old Belarius finds in subdued metaphor the language of compassion. Such passages betray an imagery in which the heart speaks more audibly than the lips.

Not only has the Sunken figure contributed to the power and poignancy of numerous lines, but much of the nervous vigor and tang of the poet's verse is indebted to it. It accentuates a thought and drives it home. Although the following figures are hardy and even harsh, they are below the level of full visualization.

> he hath strange places cramm'd
> With observation.
>
> *A. Y. L. I.* II, 7, 40

> hammer'd of this design.
>
> *W. T.* II, 2, 49

> Now swallow down that lie.
>
> *Rich. II,* I, 1, 132

> All curses madded Hecuba gave the Greeks,
> And mine to boot, be darted on thee.
>
> *Cym.* IV, 2, 313

> He that is proud eats up himself.
>
> *T. and C.* II, 3, 164

> For her own person,
> It beggar'd all description.
>
> *Ant. and Cleo.* II, 2, 202

> Which from the tongue of roaring Typhon dropp'd.
>
> *T. and C.* I, 3, 160

> Why should I write this down, that's riveted,
> Screw'd to my memory.
>
> *Cym.* II, 2, 43

To cram observation, to hammer a design, to swallow a lie, to dart a curse, to beggar description and to rivet and screw ideas in the memory are vigorous and extraordinary associations of the abstract and concrete. Energy but not moral power, distinction but not beauty characterize the lines. Without rivaling the powerful, the poignant or the elevated figures, they bear the unmistakable stamp of a masterful imagination. They have indeed much the same relation to the greater images that *Richard Third* for example bears to the great tragedies.

Sunken imagery is peculiarly adapted to an elevated and dignified language. The contemplative mind frequently shuns the more developed metaphorical forms. The stoical and speculative characters in the Roman plays often speak in subdued but seldom in Expansive or Exuberant imagery. Their metaphor is one phase of Shakespere's conception of Stoic severity. The Roman philosophy however is by no means confined to the Roman plays. Horatio is "more an antique Roman than a Dane." The following citations are therefore from a variety of sources.

> but do not stain
> The even virtue of our enterprise,
> Nor the insuppressive mettle of our spirits,
> To think that or our cause or our performance
> Did need an oath.
>> *Caesar,* II, 1, 132

> Thou art the ruins of the noblest man
> That ever lived in the tide of times.
>> *Caesar,* III, 1, 256

> A combination and a form indeed
> Where every god did seem to set his seal
> To give the world assurance of a man.
>> *Ham.* III, 4, 60

> What, girl! though grey
> Do something mingle with our younger brown, yet ha' we
> A brain that nourishes our nerves, and can
> Get goal for goal of youth.
>> *Ant. and Cleo.* IV, 8, 19

But mercy is above the sceptred sway;
It is enthroned in the hearts of kings.

M. of V. IV, 1, 193

So that the ram that batters down the wall,
For the great swing and rudeness of his poise,
They place before the hand that made the engine,
Or those that with the *fineness* of their souls
By reason guide his execution.

T. and C. I, 3, 206

Imagery in the first citation is subtly adapted to the character of Brutus. It is also a good example of the complex metaphor frequently found in this category. To stain the purity of an enterprise or to ruffle its even virtue are unmixed metaphors. The two ideas are here confused through the abundance of the poet's invention, and the figure depreciates in visibility, though not in power. The lines well show the high hand with which Shakespere treats metaphor.

The preceding figures illustrate the aid which a subtle but a subdued imagery brings to reflective poetry. In the second citation the word "ruins" has an unusual imaginative value. The corpse is not thought of in relation to some particular architectural remains. As in Spenser's title, "The Ruins of Time," thought is placed equally between concrete and abstract. It approaches the concrete, for buildings are in mind, and the abstract because the sum of all crumbling things is suggested. Much as the dead Caesar suggests to Antony the ruins of time, the mad Lear suggests to Gloucester the ruins of the future in eternity.

O ruined piece of nature! This great world
Shall so wear out to naught.

Lear, IV, 6, 137

This common Elizabethan use of the word "ruin" suggests that its meaning was at once more comprehensive and more

concrete than in our own word, which as a rule functions
to the imagination only in particulars. The capacity of
the metaphorical imagination to generalize upon the concrete and the particular is at the basis of poetic imagery.
This faculty, unusually strong in Elizabethan thought, is
supremely developed in Shakespere. In elevated poetic
metaphor the imagination may be observed to transform its
physical material into abstraction. This process is most
powerful when the idea of the physical world is spacious
and when the idea of the moral world is generous. Science expands the physical universe. An unimaginative
mind trained in the mechanical sciences, however, will be
hindered in the conception of sublime imagery. Even
more important than a generous view of time and space
and a superior understanding of natural law is the ability
to conceive vividly the changes which the physical world
undergoes. It is this capacity which appears so frequently
in Elizabethan thought and which gives the Elizabethan
poets so firm a grasp upon the sublime image in reflective
poetry. The sublime and metaphorical conception of ruin
may be contrasted with its prosaic and literal counterpart.
To Shakespere, especially in the Sonnets, all decay is a
metaphor of death or of oblivion. This is the metaphor
upon which above all others the Renaissance whetted its
imagination. The ruins of Lear are an image for the
withering of the world itself. These relations are metaphor because of the violent transition between general and
particular and between living and inanimate nature.
They belong to the Sunken category because the relation
is strongly felt, but inadequately realized in the nature of
the case. The minor term approaches an abstraction. To
the modern popular mind nourished in business and industry buildings crumble, flowers wither, men die, but the
common mutability of all things is less strongly realized.
A change in religious ideas has altered all conceptions of

mortality. Nevertheless, as the five remaining citations in the last group indicate, the comprehensive image in the field of moral ideas reached an extraordinary development in Elizabethan poetry, not appreciable to the man in the street to-day, and for which a change in religious ideas cannot account. This poetry was popular. It was in the popular drama that phrases such as "ripeness is all" appeared. Not the intellectual class alone but the people seem in a large measure to have spoken and enjoyed the language of a poetic philosophy. This language may be read in the metaphor of "stain" for a moral blemish, of an "even" virtue for an unfluctuating one, of a divine "seal" for a divine assurance, of the "goals" of life for the fulfillment of happiness, of an enthronement for mercy in the heart, and of the "fineness" of edges for the fineness of intellects. It does not follow that the mind which sees life in generous proportions will possess a keen metaphorical gift. Far less does it follow that a keen metaphorical gift implies such a vision. There is however a probability that the imaginative perception of ideals will exist most generally in a period which shows some gift for the comprehensive metaphor. This problem will receive increasing attention as the more developed forms of metaphor are discussed.

Before passing to other poets than Shakespere let us consider what a supreme image of the present category may signify composed by the master of the form. The metaphor which I select as a type is in structure fully representative. It inclines rather toward literalness than toward another category. This line is from the Chorus to the Fourth Act of *Henry Fifth*.

A little touch of Harry in the night.

To quote this out of its context without some exposition is impossible. Shakespere describes the effect of the young

King passing in cheerful disguise among his troops before the first light of day glimmers over the field of Agincourt. After the battle there will be wounds to bind and an enemy to pursue. Meanwhile as that inevitable event draws nearer human nature is passing through a supreme trial. Then if ever there is need of some Harry to assert even in the darkest hour whatever nobility is or may be in man. Harry on the night of Agincourt is a metaphor of the poet among his fellow men. Shakespere's hint of metaphor is in no slight degree responsible for the effectiveness of the line.

Some figures follow from other poets, which further illustrate the particular adaptation of restrained imagery to elevated thought.

> And that unless above himself he can
> Erect himself, how poor a thing is man.
> > Daniel, *Epistle to Lady Margaret*

> But God forbid we should so nearly pry
> Into the low-deep-buried sins long past.
> > Daniel, *Civil Wars,* I, 97

> Shall we not offer to thy excellence
> The richest treasures that our wit affords.
> > Daniel, *Musophilus*

> You mighty lords that in respected grace
> Do at the stem of fair example stand,
> And all the body of this populace
> Guide as with the turning of your hand,
> Keep a straight course; bear up from all disgrace;
> Observe the point of honor to our land.
> > Daniel, *Musophilus*

> For ever who in derring doe were dread
> The lofty verse of hem was loved aye.
> > Sp. *S. C.* X, 65

She hath the bonds broke of eternal night,
Her soul unbodied of the burdenous corpse.
Sp. *S. C.* XI, 165

(a hill)
gives the eye lordship over a good large circuit.
Sidney, *Arcadia,* I, 62

A reaching heart will search his deepest wits
And cast with cunning for the time to come.
Marlowe, *Jew of Malta,* I, 2

The wonderous architecture of the world.
Marlowe, *I Tamb.,* II, 7, 22

The character of Daniel is a comment not only on his own imagery but on the humanistic significance of reserved metaphor. He is a man who without the highest literary attainments shows exceptional moral dignity, modesty, and grace. Without striving for effect, for notoriety or for a reputation of wit, without brilliancy as a thinker and without the more passionate notes of poetry, his generous vision, his urbanity and his rectitude insure him at least the honor if not the glory of literary fame. Such a man is inclined by temperament toward a subdued imagery. Recognized as a writer in the classical style he shuns exuberant metaphor. In his sonnets his restraint keeps him from a free use of the Decorative image and disinclines him from excess in the Radical form. In *Hymen's Triumph,* his idyllic masque, scarcely an extravagant figure appears. Expressions of his refined stoicism are frequently cast in subdued metaphor. Such language is conspicuous in his masterpiece, *Musophilus,* a poem on university education still remembered in those English-speaking countries remote from England to which he prophesied that English literature would come. By this type of imagery the poet stimulates the imagination of the reader to rise to his powerful, liberal

and prophetic thought. Like Bacon, Daniel was impelled
to a vision of the future by a noble and metaphorical imagination, but where Bacon's figures show the Elizabethan
daring Daniel's are always dignified and restrained. Bacon's are in the language of intellectual enthusiasm, Daniel's in the language of moral discrimination. Shakespere,
Milton and Wordsworth excepted, few English poets suggest a more interesting use of subdued imagery.—In a very
different context appear the figures cited above from Marlowe. Those from *The Shepherd's Calendar* suggest Milton, who also wrote of "the lofty rhyme." Though Sidney's image may suggest the salt of an Arcadian conceit
it possesses, I believe, nobility and restraint.

The following citations illustrate how poets other than
Shakespere express an unusual poignancy in Sunken metaphor.

> Why do we longer live; ah, why live we so long;
> Whose better days death hath shut up in woe?
>> Sp. *S. C.* XI, 73

> Ah, they been all yclad in clay,
> One bitter blast blew all away.
>> Ib. XI, 118

> You frame my thoughts and fashion me within;
> You stop my tongue and teach my heart to speak.
>> Sp. *Amoretti,* 8

> Two knights that linked rode in lovely wise.
>> *Fairie Queene,* IV, 2, 30

> And wiping out remembrance of all ill
> Grant him your grace.
>> Ib. IV, 6, 32

> What greater joy can any man desire
> Than to remain a captive unto love.
>> *England's Helicon,* 87

Let me home return stark blinded
Of those eyes, and blinder minded.
      Astrophel and Stella, Song 8

A naked thinking heart that makes no show
Is to a woman but a kind of ghost.
      Donne, *The Blossom*

For these lines are the veins, the arteries
And undecaying life-strings of those hearts.
      Daniel, *Musophilus*

The imagery of these poignant lines is too delicate to brook
criticism.

IV

THE VIOLENT IMAGE OR FUSTIAN

In Violent imagery, or metaphorical fustian, imagination is restricted by sensationalism, which reduces to a minimum the intellectual elements of the figure, by impetuosity, which blurs the relation of the terms, and by a prevailing conventionality, which hinders a close adjustment of the figure to a particular case. These statements may serve at once for a concise description and for an outline of a large part of the present chapter. No extended description is needed to convey the significance of the form. From the Cleon of Aristophanes to the modern campaign speech fustian has been a god in the affairs of men. It has elected candidates, brought armies to blows, frightened poetry from the popular stage, and has seemed to vanquish death itself as an instrument of the eulogist. Decorative imagery, or the conceit, gave amusement to a handful of aristocratic Elizabethans. It was a vice of no more than a frolic pedantry. Sunken imagery is too fine and Radical imagery too intricate to be popular. Intensive and Expansive imagery, for the most part metaphors of beauty and idealism, are intimations of an ideal world. Fustian is a monarch of this world. It is therefore of some interest to observe by what means it monarchizes over the opinions and emotions of men.

Fustian may itself be broadly described as linguistic exhilaration for its own sake. It is grounded in egoism. It flourishes in oratory because the position of the orator, with a crowd intent upon his words and gestures, is favorable to the egoist. The speaker cares more for his effect than for his theme. While apparently rapt in his subject he is actu-

100

ally ensphered in his own glory. His language then is at bottom vulgar and bears no affinity to poetry.

The metaphor of fustian falls in point of form into two types, more nearly allied than would at first appear. Its bolder images are eccentric. Its milder figures strike the imagination with the same jar that platitudes give the reason. They are "pat," as in the slang use of "lid" for hat. But though the image is pat it is anything but subtly adjusted. It shows in its own way the usual carelessness of Violent speech.

In this figure less is meant than meets the ear. It attains a fine point of efficiency. There is only one possible interpretation. The author commands obedience. His language rings loud and clear so that he who runs must comprehend. We are not induced to finer thought or finer feeling but spurred to immediate and violent action or vanquished by a shamefully simple emotion. The appeal is instantaneous and sensational, never subtle or contemplative. In figures of a grossly sensational character there will of necessity be less imaginative activity than in those which leave the door of philosophy ajar. Consider for example two figures alike in their nominal subject but otherwise unlike. One is thrilling and sensational. The other arouses an almost illimitable play of fancy and of the reflective faculties. One is Violent, the other Expansive. The first is in Shakespere's earliest manner, the second in his latest.

> Methought I saw a thousand fearful wrecks,
> A thousand men that fishes gnaw'd upon,
> Wedges of gold, great anchors, heaps of pearl,
> Inestimable stones, unvalued jewels,
> All scattered in the bottom of the sea.
> Some lay in dead men's skulls; and in the hole
> Where eyes did once inhabit, there were crept,
> As 'twere in scorn of eyes, reflecting gems,

That woo'd the slimy bottom of the deep,
And mock'd the dead bones that lay scatter'd by.
                                        Rich. III, I, 4, 24

Full fathom five thy father lies,
Of his bones are coral made;
Those are pearls that were his eyes;
Nothing in him that doth fade
But doth suffer a sea change
Into something rich and strange.
                                        Tem. I, 2, 396

The charnel house terrors of the earlier lines strike powerfully upon the naïve mind. A sophisticated mind may
perhaps enter a state sympathetic with such sensations. If
the lights are turned on however an artificial setting is
shown essential to an enjoyment of so ghastly a picture.
On the contrary the aesthetic and moral suggestiveness of
the celebrated lines from *The Tempest* make them not a
violent experience but a permanent possession. If their
phrasing is forgotten it is lost only as the seed is lost in the
plant. Their thought, in Hazlitt's words, "slides into the
current of our blood." The foremost characteristic of this
type of imagery is not its vagueness but its power. By the
romantic critics, as for example by Wordsworth, imagination is frequently distinguished as vague and fancy as precise in its outline. Thus eyes of pearl would be fancy,
while the transformation of the entire body into "something rich and strange" would be imagination. As previously intimated this distinction seems itself somewhat more
vague than imaginative. Mystification may in excess have
more a nullifying than a stimulating effect. The lines in
The Tempest are imaginatively effective not so much because they are indefinite as because they powerfully employ
imagery in behalf of reflection. Their first appeal is to
the fancy, aroused by the idea of opalescent color. Only

the bones of the King are coral. The rest of him is of an
unknown element. The impression is that "coral" itself
is figurative for those exquisitely various parts of innumerable dyes into which the body is transformed. Finally
comes the decisive metaphor. As the sea itself like a divine opal is in restless and perpetual change, the body
which sinks into it becomes an equally unstable part of
eternal beauty. The fancy of Ariel leads us from delight
to meditation. The suggestion of these lines is that Shakespere finds the laws of nature which make and unmake man
not just in the one and evil in the other but one law in
the pursuit of august and inevitable change. A human life
is an episode in the greater life of nature. The consequence of this thought is to dignify life and to reconcile
life to death. These lines then possess a far different value
from those in *Richard Third*. The latter cause at most
only a passing shudder. One passage represents Expansive imagery, the other Violent. The highest imaginative
value in metaphor exists only when the mind is carried
away by a particular scene to the comprehension of a wide
range of suggestions. This condition is most generously
fulfilled when the figure contains the germ of contemplation.
A man pursued by a bull will have a lively picture of impending calamity. His imagination will leap at whatever
offers a desperate hope of relief. The sensation of fear and
an impulsive grasp for safety will be the limits of his ideas.
There will be no more art in his imagination than philosophy in his thought. Great metaphor neither arises from
such experiences nor portrays them. It is not sensational.
It qualifies pleasure, distinguishes pain and modifies ideas.

The lack of condensation in much of the language of
fustian metaphor is not of course peculiar to that type of
imagery or to fustian itself. Nothing however can more
readily be observed about a figure than the number of

words to which it is extended. The redundant style of the
citation from *Richard Third*, "inestimable stones, unvalued
jewels," is in contrast with the pregnant language of Ariel.
Consider three metaphorical ideas each treated in the expanded and condensed style, belonging to Violent imagery
when expanded and to the higher categories when condensed. In Kyd's *Spanish Tragedy* Hieronimo soliloquizes
thus:

> Yet still tormented is my tortured soul
> With broken sighs and restless passions,
> That winged mount and hovering in the air
> Beat at the windows of the highest heavens
> Soliciting for justice and revenge.
>
> III, 7, 10

This is a varied form of the same image.

> Haply I think on thee; and then my state,
> Like to the lark at break of day arising
> From sullen earth, sings hymns at heaven's gate.
>
> *Son.* 29

In Kyd "tormented" and "tortured," "broken sighs" and
"restless passions," "justice" and "revenge" are virtual
repetitions. The two lines that comprise the kernel of the
figure seem beaten thin when contrasted with the packed
language of Shakespere. The distinction is between blind
impetuosity, which forbids the finer poetic metaphor, and
intense lyric passion expressed through the chastening
medium of art. In *Richard Second* we read,

> A jewel in a ten-times-barr'd up chest
> Is a bold spirit in a loyal breast.
>
> I, 1, 180

In *Othello* we read,

> Good name in man or woman, dear my Lord,
> Is the immediate jewel of their souls.
>
> III, 3, 155

In the earlier play, written with an inexhaustible enthusiasm, the jewel is placed in a "ten-time's-barr'd up chest." In one play the metaphor takes a line, in the other a single word. Balanced rhetoric, inevitably expanded, and a mouth-filling compound contrast with easy but pregnant language. In Shakespere's later plays where a figure in the full imaginative manner extends over several lines it contains as a rule nothing that can be omitted without seriously damaging the effect. Though it is impossible to paraphrase Shakespere's later imagery without considerable extension, the gist of his earlier imagery may often be given in briefer form. Shakespere himself crams a line of *Richard Second* into a word in *Othello*.

In Greene we read,

> . . . To scud and overscour the world in post
> Upon the speedy wings of swiftest winds.
>
> *Friar Bacon,* 1967

In Shakespere we should, I think, have simply the epithet "winged." Greene's language is grossly inflated. "Scud," "overscour," "in post," "wings" or even "winds" might alone carry a heavier metaphorical burden than all five words together, yet these five figurative words are superfluously supported by the epithets "speedy" and "swiftest." Although the mark of inflated language does not enter strictly into a description of a type of metaphor, it serves to illustrate the underlying idea of impetuosity and may be regarded as an introduction and a sign.

When the world of the creative writer is full of prodigy and confusion, not of light that as if by miracle changes the doubtful and dark into the intelligible and the beautiful, we conclude that the writer is inspired by a mere frenzy, not by the fine frenzy of the poet. So pathetic fallacies of the most desperate description are abundantly represented in the early Elizabethan drama.

O worthy sir, my cause but slightly known
May move the hearts of warlike Myrmidons,
And melt the Corsick rocks with ruthful tears.
                Kyd, *Spanish Tragedy*, III, 13, 70

E'er Arthur lands the sea shall blush with blood,
And all the strands with smooking slaughter reek.
            Hughes, *Misfortunes of Arthur*, I, 4, 124

Yet Aeolus would not be a murderer,
But left that hateful office unto thee.
The pretty-vaulting sea refus'd to drown me,
Knowing that thou wouldst have me drown'd on shore,
With tears as salt as sea, through thy unkindness.
The splitting rocks cower'd in the sinking sands
And would not dash me with their ragged sides,
Because thy flinty heart, more hard than they,
Might in thy palace perish Margaret.
                II Hen. VI, III, 2, 92

The images from *The Spanish Tragedy* and *The Misfortunes of Arthur* are equally conventional and preposterous. Of the several illustrations of Violent metaphor in the lines cited from the Second Part of *Henry Sixth* that of most immediate interest is the pathetic fallacy in lines 97–98. The figure may be contrasted with a nominally similar one in *Othello*.

Tempests themselves, high seas, and howling winds,
The gutter'd rocks and congregated sands,
Traitors ensteeped to clog the guiltless keel,
As having sense of beauty, do omit
Their mortal natures, letting go safely by
The divine Desdemona.

                                    II, 1, 68

When the material world is in tumult and what we best love and admire in peril it is fully within the bounds of normal imagination to picture an ideal world, where beauty overawes nature and passes by unscathed.

> The powers aboon will tent thee;
> Misfortune sha'na steer thee;
> Thou'rt like themselves sae lovely
> That ill they'll ne're let near thee.

The misstatement of nature is more than justified by the veracity with which Shakespere and Burns express the longings of all hearts. Metaphorical fustian cannot be described or condemned as a violation of fact. Lines of exquisite imaginative value do the same. The lines in The Second Part of *Henry Sixth* are perilously near fustian not because the pathetic fallacy of rocks cowering from the wicked Queen is in bold violation of nature, but because the image violates nature ruthlessly and without a revealing comment on human life. The frenzied poet is ranging at random through the elements. A period of such extreme storm and stress in imagery may perhaps have its place in the education of a poet. Most readers however will hold that the image from *Henry Sixth*, by whomsoever the passage may have been written, like the two images from Hughes and Kyd, is a blemish. The figure from *Othello* on the contrary may be taken as a consummation of art fashioning the world to the heart's desire.

No less startling than this violent animism is the violent and impetuous hyperbole. These are typical illustrations from the early drama.

> Ah, now I feel the paper told me true;
> The poison is disperst through every vein,
> And boils like Etna in my frying guts.
>> Kyd, *Soliman and Perseda,* V, 4, 144

> I will stir up in England some black storm
> Shall blow ten thousand souls to heaven or hell.
>> *II Hen. VI,* III, 1, 349

> . . . Whose sorrows lay more siege unto my soul
> Than all my armies to Damascus' walls.
>> Marlowe, *I, Tamb.* V, 2, 92

Like many of the Violent figures in early tragedy the citation from Kyd will probably appear coarse to a modern
reader. The images from The Second Part of *Henry Sixth*
and from *Tamburlaine* seem above common fustian but in
imaginative value far below many figures in the same plays.

At times a strong incongruity between fully visualized
terms in diffuse language typifies figures in the present
category. The following are not merely bold, but show an
abandon hardly reconcilable with the finer daring of mature art.

> Ay, kennel, puddle, sink, whose filth and dirt
> Troubles the silver spring where England drinks,
> Now will I dam up thy yawning mouth
> For swallowing the treasure of the realm.
>
> *II Hen. VI,* IV, 1, 71

> And for we think the eagle-winged pride
> Of sky aspiring and ambitious thoughts
> With rival-bating envy, set on you
> To wake our peace, which in our country's cradle
> Draws the sweet infant breath of gentle sleep. . . .
>
> *Rich. II,* I, 3, 129

> O would to God that the inclusive verge
> Of golden mettle that must round my brow
> Were red-hot steel to seer me to the brains.
>
> *Rich. III,* IV, 1, 59

The violent incongruity in the first citation is perhaps
greatest, in the second less and in the third least. None of
the images however is, I believe, quite in the manner of a
purified art.

Of all the passions none is expressed more readily in
Violent metaphor than anger. Contemplation and the
sympathetic prospect of beauty are equally removed from
anger and from fustian. Indignation may indeed be stimulating to the highest imagination. The wrath of the proph-

ets and the wrath of Dante are couched in lofty metaphor.
When however a coarse mind loses its control anger expresses itself in such dramatic images as these.

> Hence, heap of wrath, foul, indigested lump,
> As crooked in thy manners as thy shape.
>> *II Hen. VI*, V, 1, 157

> Thou elvish-mark'd, abortive, rooting hog!
>> *Rich. III*, 1, 3, 228

> Why strew'st thou sugar on that bottl'd spider?
>> Ib. 242

> Look, when he fawns, he bites; and when he bites
> His venom tooth will rankle to the death.
>> Ib. 290

Such are the injurious metaphors which the enemies of
Richard strew upon him in their hatred. This is in the
contemptuous spirit.

> She's tickled now; her fume needs not spurs;
> She'll gallop far enough to her destruction.
>> *II Hen. VI*, 1, 3, 153

In the metaphor of anger expression is formless and impetuous. In the metaphor of indignation expression shows
the discipline of art.—It need scarcely be said however that
with Shakespere the dramatic character of the speaker
should be considered.

With images of anger are associated the numerous re-
volting figures in Elizabethan drama. Disagreeable as
they are, they have occasionally a power surprising to those
accustomed to gentler language; they are by no means ig-
noble. An illustration may be taken from The Second
Part of *Henry Fourth*.

> For the fifth Harry from curb'd licence plucks
> The muzzle of restraint, and the wild dog
> Shall flesh his tooth in every innocent.
>> IV, 5, 131

Another passion which like anger checks contemplation and a sympathetic prospect of the beautiful is terror. The large number of charnel house figures, especially in the early melodrama, well illustrates the type. Despairing it would seem of satisfying the audience by bloody scenes or by bloody dialogue alone, the dramatists punctuated their language with metaphorical skulls and daggers. Something more than action and straightforward talk was needed to sustain the level of

> Tragedia cothurnata, fitting kings,
> Containing matter, and not meaner things!

The number of casualties physically possible on the stage was deplorably low. But by metaphor bravely declaimed every horror could be augmented an hundred fold. Even in *Coriolanus,* the last and one of the soberest of Shakespere's tragedies from the standpoint of metaphor, images occur which though transcending the earlier manner suggest it. Though there are no casualties in the third act of that great play these lines are worth a thousand.

> The fires i' the lowest hell fold in the people!
> Call me their traitor! Thou injurious tribune!
> Within thy eyes set twenty thousand death's,
> In thy hands clutch'd as many millions, in
> Thy lying tongue both numbers, I would say
> "Thou liest" unto thee with a voice as free
> As I do pray the gods!

> > > > > > > III, 3, 68

Coriolanus' passion for aristocracy is here an unusually vexed compound of indignation and anger. A masculine love of horror which developed into the magnificent curses of Lear and Coriolanus had its origin in the terrors of the early melodrama.

Much as it is the tendency of all blindly impetuous persons to go out of the straight road, the use of the Violent

image is bound to become at times self-destructive, and
digressive. It strikes wildly, misses aim and becomes eccentric. In the Violent figure emphasis is frequently
thrown upon the minor term, as in The Second Part of
Henry Sixth:

> Gloucester's show
> Beguiles him as the mournful crocodile
> With sorrow snares relenting passengers,
> Or as the snake roll'd in a flow'ring bank
> With shining checker'd slough, doth sting a child
> That for its beauty thinks it excellent.
>
> III, 1, 225

Doubtless the poet and his audience took immense pleasure
in these mournful, glittering and guileful beasts. So much
so indeed that the crocodile and the snake seem temporarily
to receive more attention than the deceitful Gloucester,
whose wiles they are nominally to exemplify.

Melodrama, the sensational story and the declamatory
address, the principal sources for fustian, are marked by
strong conventionality. Their art is not therefore less
sincere. The ideas and emotions of street orators and sensational writers are notably restricted. Relatively few
varieties of terror and anger for example are known to
them. Consequently terror may on all occasions "petrify"
and anger "boil." The figures are "pat." In no respect
is sensational literature more conventional than in its
metaphors. The greater the dramatic poet the less likely
he is to repeat himself. If his observation is keen and his
expression adequate, characters and situations will seldom
be reduplicated, and metaphors will be appropriately
shaded to all changes of circumstance and emotion. Even
guild images of the religious poet and the lyric idealist are
subtly altered, although the alterations are on the surface
scarcely perceptible. Today only the sensationalist shame-
lessly repeats himself. In certain early literatures only is

the frank repetition of a stock of images found in poetry of recognized merit. The reiterated figures in Homer are for example the metaphorical anthology of a race that could afford to be repetitious. When however fustian images are repeated whether in the sixteenth or the twentieth century the sophisticated intruder will smile where pity or indignation is intended. So these figures, which are among the numerous conventions in the early Elizabethan tragedy of blood, the modern reader is likely to find naïve and mildly risible.

> So striveth not the waves with sundry winds
> As Fortune toileth in affairs of kings.
>> Kyd, *Spanish Tragedy*, III, 1, 8

> *Then I unclasp the purple leaves of war;*
> Many a new wound must gasp through an old scar.
>> Kyd, *Hieronimo*, Part I, I, 1, 87

> Now, Madame, since by favor of your love
> Our hidden smoke is turned to open flame,
>> Kyd, *Spanish Tragedy*, II, 2, 1

> Like as the craggy rock
> Resists the streams, and flings the weltering waves
> Aloof, so he rejects and scorns my words.
>> Hughes, *Misfortunes of Arthur*, II, 3, 152

> A huge aspiring rock neighboring the skies,
> Whose surly brow imperiously commands
> The sea his bounds, that at his proud feet lie.
>> Daniel, *Civil Wars*, II, 48

> They that stand high have many blasts to shake them,
> And when they fall they dash themselves to pieces.
>> *Rich. III*, I, 3, 259

The greater number of metaphors in the tragedies suggest Seneca, the chief classical source of inspiration for the new dramatists. These are in the once much admired Senecan style.

What are thy tears but Circe's magic seas
Where none scape wreck but blindfold mariners.
Soliman and Perseda, II, 1, 157

Or like the snaky wreath of Tisiphon
Ingirt the temple of his hateful head.
Soliman and Perseda, V, 1, 45

Like a foul Gorgon, whose dishevelled hair
With every blast flies glaring in the air.
Drayton, *Heroical Epistles, Elinor Cobham*

Thus, while the vulture of sedition
Feeds in the bosom of such great commanders,
Sleeping neglection doth betray to loss.
I Hen. VI, IV, 3, 47

Such figures of blood, derived from classical sources, were exposed to parrotlike repetition. Conventional images accorded with conventional scenes. The earlier Elizabethans were scarcely aware in art of that inexhaustible variety of life which is the goal of their mature drama.

The subjective or interpretative element necessary for poetic imagery has fullest scope in figures which relate the outer world of nature to the inner world of man. Much Violent imagery relates the physical to the physical world without finer shades of interpretation. In any review of the early tragedy scores of such conventional metaphors will be found. Here are some typical lines from Kyd, which liken shot in a battle to an angry ocean.

While they maintain hot skirmish to and fro
Both battles join and fall to bandy blows,
Their violent shot resembling th' ocean's rage
When roaring loud and with a swelling tide
It beats upon the rampiers of huge rocks,
And gaps to swallow neighbor bounding lands.
Spanish Tragedy, I, 2, 46

The figure selected to stand as the final illustration of the preceding category was from *Henry Fifth*. Even more typical of the imagery of that play as a whole and admirably typical of the Violent metaphor are the italicized lines of the King.

> For there is none of you so mean and base
> That hath not noble lustre in your eyes.
> *I see you stand like greyhounds in the slips,*
> *Straining upon the start! The game's afoot!*
> Follow your spirit, and upon this charge
> Cry "God for Harry, England and Saint George!"
>
> III, 1, 29

With Violent images arising from the sensations of anger and terror we have associated those that incite the crowd, that are the weapons of the moment wielded often with pain, and that are barren of beauty or contemplation, those passports to poetry and the ideal. Such a figure is Hal's too celebrated metaphor of the greyhounds. Shakespere places these words in the mouth of the King at the crucial moment before a charge. To the moral influence of the King Shakespere seems to attribute much of the success of his forces. The young leader is here arousing himself to a supreme effort. These last words which are to send his troops against the enemy are an ideal instance of the Violent metaphor. Such imagination drives men forward on the spur of the moment. It is not the profoundly poetic image under the inspiration of which men live and by which philosophy holds its torch to the masses of mankind. These nobler images are such as Shakespere's own "ripeness is all" and the metaphors of Bacon and of Burke.

Leaving the analysis and illustration of the Violent image behind we may now proceed to frame the picture and summarize the significance of the form. In few instances is the evolution of a type of metaphor so fascinating as in the case of this category during the lifetime of Shakespere. Beginning with the first years of the Elizabethan period the development may readily be traced by reference to representative plays. It is a story of the importation of artificial, pseudo-Senecan conventions, of the ascendency of these conventions in the early tragedy, and of the gradual relaxing of the stiffness and the liberation of the vitality which the early images contain. The type originates in a foreign literary convention, becomes animated by native talent, its fustian and bombast become generous enthusiasm and robust poetry, until at the touch of the greater poets the old manner totally disappears. While the Violent image occurs sporadically in the Jacobean drama, its supremacy was by the end of the sixteenth century irrevocably lost. Apart from such occasional heroic and patriotic verse as the historical poems of Drayton and Daniel the tradition rose, flourished and declined in the drama.

Omitting the dumb show, the early tragedy contained relatively little metaphor. But what there was was largely in "King Cambyses' vein." Hyperboles, pathetic fallacies, eccentricities, creaking clumsiness and above all conventionality typify the figures. This description applies to metaphor in *Gorboduc*. Perhaps no aspect of that impressive and deeply serious play, which plead for the unification of Elizabeth's England, seems to the modern reader so archaic as its imagery. One of the most extended and vigorous figurative passages is the following.

> Thou never suckt the milk of human breast
> But from thy birth the cruel tiger's teats
> Have nursed thee, nor yet of flesh and blood
> Formed is thy heart, but of hard iron wrought.
>
> IV, 1, 72

In Gascoigne's *Jocasta* the stiffness of the older figures is somewhat relaxed. *Gismund of Salerne,* one of the most notable English tragedies of love before *Romeo and Juliet,* is thinly sown with metaphors but what figures there are though mostly Violent show a riper imagination than those in *Jocasta*. Horrors are more convincing and less rhetorical. Nowhere is fustian more naïve than in the tragedy of *Locrine*. Somewhat later and more inspired is the Violent imagery in such plays as *Selimus* and *Caesar's Revenge*.

Marlowe's images have for the most part a far higher value than the present category allows. His poetry is the foremost source for the Exuberant metaphor of beauty. If many of his figures might be called Violent, they are much more as well. They are not mere declamation or fustian. In their beauty they are the antithesis of the coarse. Though metaphorical relations are not precise the images are often magnificent, even sublime. The pure gold of the figures of *Tamburlaine* cannot be mistaken for the baser metal. When Marlowe descends from his peak which no English poet could scale or chose to scale but he, a Violent image may occasionally be observed. It is unnecessary to record these apparent stumblings. The important fact is his break with the older metaphorical tradition. With his love of beauty, his fine daring and high sensuousness he liberated imagination from the bands of fustian. When the public became aware that there were more "thrills" to be had from the figures of poetry than from the figures of melodrama, raw sensationalism was discarded. Marlowe spoke its doom. His two associates, Peele and Greene, also broke with the pseudo-Senecan tradition. Peele seems on the whole more prolific of the new forms than Greene.

The early histories of Shakespere bristle with metaphorical ferocities. In these plays and in *Titus Andronicus* figures quite as often suggest the classical tradition as the new imagery of Marlowe. Of all plays in the Shakespere canon the most impoverished in sympathetic imagery is The First Part of *Henry Sixth*. The Second Part on the contrary contains many figures that rise well above sensation-

alism. From the standpoint of metaphor Act Three stands
in the Trilogy in splendid isolation. Here are many figures that suggest the powerful epithets for the "wolfish
barons" in Marlowe's *Edward II*. The Third Part of
Henry Sixth shows Violent metaphors of the cruder sort.
There are however some deviations. The conceited language of the unhappy King, for example, shows a digression from Violent imagery. The latter form reaches its
height in *Richard Third*. Here although the figures are
powerful they are for the most part without high imaginative value. They are sensational, impetuous, exaggerated
but usually conventional. Anger can scarcely be more
vigorously expressed in metaphor than in the impreca-
tions of the unfortunate women against the usurper. The
only difficulty for the modern reader is to stomach the allusions bursting forth with almost volcanic profusion in
Margaret's curse. While Lear and Coriolanus find a noble
language of imprecation, the language of this Queen is de-
filing. There is not even the irresistible sweep and energy
of Macbeth's "The devil damn thee black, thou cream
faced loon!" (V, 3, 11). Margaret's images are the sput-
tering of venomous wrath, Macbeth's a satanic poetry.

In *Richard Second*, metaphor is rapidly divorcing itself
from sensationalism. What was merely a loud manner
ceases to be harsh and becomes brilliant. Richard himself
is a man whose prevailing curse is to look upon the world
evasively through the spectacles of forced metaphor. In
contrast are his nobles. Their ardent spirits burn into a
flame of dazzling imagery which illumines the entire play.
They employ metaphor as an exercise, like arms, appropriate to nobility. At court all plain language is thought
dull witted and plebeian. The alternative however is not
the trifling, Decorative incongruities which abound in
Love's Labor's Lost, but the ardent symbol-making of
youth that takes life as a tournament. The play affords a
picture of an aristocracy of reckless self-expression in the

metaphorical word as well as in the warlike deed. Shakespere celebrates a liberation from a bare, ferocious and almost primitive age, revealed in the pseudo-Senecan tragedies and a century before dominant in England. In depicting the crimes of the wolfish barons Violent metaphor
was not inappropriate. The poet under such circumstances might well sink himself in his subject. *Richard
Second* flashes with a new spirit, both more sensuous and
more intellectual. A new imagery becomes essential. No
play shows more prodigality, rapidity, breathlessness and
"insolence." The metaphors gallop like a troop of horse
in a spring pasture. Their abundance gives assurance of
new power. Their originality shows that the conventions
of the pseudo-Senecan tradition need no longer be a re-
course. Their joyousness proves that the poet will no
longer condescend to thrill an audience with mere blood
and terror, but will delight with the poetry of beauty and
idealism. If Shakespere's best imagery is by no means
attained in *Richard Second,* he has turned his back on the
old ways. Here for example is a typical figure standing
between sensationalism and poetry. It occurs in the defiance scene in Act One, where heaped up figures resemble
in martial splendor those highly decorated coats of mail or
that brilliant flourish of trumpets which are imagined to
accompany the action.

> Never did captive with a freer heart
> Cast off his chains of bondage and embrace
> His golden uncontroll'd infranchisement,
> More than my dancing soul doth celebrate
> This feast of battle with mine adversary.

> I, 3, 88

A subtle dramatic development in the images of Richard
himself may be seen in the last act, when a life of vanity
closes in a quiet evening of revelation. Akin to the general imagery of this play, it may be remarked, is that of

The Rape of Lucrece, and that too little known poem, *Drake,* by Charles FitzGeoffry.

In the preceding pages several illustrations of Violent images have been drawn from the two Parts of *Henry Fourth,* and from *Henry Fifth.* In the First Part of *Henry Fourth* Marlowe's lyrical manner of sowing figures indiscriminately among his speakers yields to a strictly dramatic technique. Each character speaks in finely appropriate imagery. The Exuberant figures of Hotspur, the mystical imagery of Glendower and the formal Decorative metaphor of the King are appropriate to character. Violent figures are much less frequent than in earlier plays. In the Second Part the number of sensational figures is larger. *Henry Fifth* and *King John* are no more consistent from the standpoint of imagery than from the standpoint of dramatic unity. In each play a considerable number of violent metaphors may be found. In both plays, especially in *Henry Fifth,* there are however figures of a poetic elevation to which little if anything comparable can be found in the plays previously referred to.

This gradual decline of Violent imagery traced in a few selected plays of Shakespere's may be taken as representative of the poetry of the period. With the later Jacobean drama all forms of imagery decreased, but none so rapidly as this. An interesting contrast occurs between the Violent imagery of the sixteenth century tragedy and of the English Heroical Drama of the Age of Dryden. The early Elizabethans wrote sensational figures because a sensational exercise of the imagination was the web and woof of their existence. In this metaphor they exercised the full man. The writers of the English Heroical Drama inflated their style with sensational figures because a literary exercise in metaphorical imagination, the more violent the better, stimulated an otherwise neglected factor in their vigorous but not highly imaginative culture. The whole man speaks in Mowbray's words,

> my dancing soul doth celebrate
> This feast of battle with mine adversary.

Of a different sort are such forced images as these.

> As some fair tulip by a storm oppressed
> Shrinks up and folds its silken arms to rest,
> And bending to the blast all pale and dread
> Hears from within the wind sing round its head,
> So shrouded up your beauty disappears;
> Unveil, my love, and lay aside your fears.
>
> *The Conquest of Granada,* I, 5

There is more naturalness in the audacity of Mowbray's imagination than in the elaborate, rotund and relatively plausible image from Dryden. The metaphors of the Heroical Drama are not so foreign to external nature as the Elizabethan extravagances. These extravagances however are much nearer to the hearts of the sincere poets who composed them than the images of the heroical plays are to their poets. An Elizabethan metaphor of Violence is in short less consistent within itself but more consistent with its creator.

This category of relatively low imaginative value has been treated at length first because by contrast it throws light on higher forms of imagery; at any period it comprises a large and socially important body of metaphor; and finally an historical view of this category in Elizabethan literature shows a simple and rapid transformation of sensational figures into the mature poetic metaphors of the early Jacobean tragedy. The form might be observed in the verse romances of Byron, written before the great satirist had spoken. It may be found in that admirable parody, Aytoun's *Firmilian.* It might be seen in the last sensational novel of the day. Nowhere however can the lineal development of a sincere melodramatic imagery into exalted poetry be traced with greater ease than in Elizabethan literature.

V

THE RADICAL IMAGE

In Radical imagery the minor term is itself of little imaginative value but the metaphorical relation is powerful.

Many objects quite apart from figurative suggestiveness stimulate imagination. These are clearly objects of some artistic consequence. Such are the typical materials of poetic imagery. More especially the poets of the eighteenth century held that dignified matter alone is fit for similes in verse. The language of an entire poem was placed upon a classic pedestal, lifted above the noise and dust of the street. A prescribed formality increased as inspiration grew colder. Inconsistently enough with this practice in metaphor, it was often decreed that the subject of a poem should be familiar to the daily life of the poet and his readers. A fit language was sought to elevate essentially undignified thoughts of persons and events. No simpler means than heroic metaphor or comparison was available. In Victorian verse the formality of an Aaron Hill was largely dispensed with. Yet while imagery became easier and less conventional, it was still governed by a rigid propriety. Few vulgar or unlovely or seemingly trivial objects were permissible. The sublimity of stars and the beauty of roses were the tests for metaphor. A commonplace subject for an image in serious verse would have disgusted and surprised the reader like grit in a smooth and delicate food. The Elizabethan style, to which more recent poetry seems increasingly to return, utilized in imagery the most familiar objects. The ugly can never be made in itself beautiful nor the trivial sublime, but the metaphorical mind may abstract from the unlovely and the trivial highly suggestive elements. The process inclines to ingenuity. It borders upon wit. Nevertheless Radical imagery has played an honorable part in reflective poetry generally and especially in English literature of the early seventeenth century.

Although the mind of Donne seems the impersonation of Radical imagery, it is with some hestitation that I have selected him for special attention in this chapter. To continue to view him from the standpoint of his imagery is to contribute to a somewhat overworked vein of criticism. Donne did much more than master and perhaps at times abuse the Radical figure. The first four of his five *Satires, The Progress of the Soul,* the larger part of his well-known *Anniversaries* and much of his religious poetry, as for example his masterpiece, *A Hymn to God the Father,* are, if our definition is carefully considered, practically without instances of this style. Donne seldom writes without subordinating not only his imagery as such but the entire manner of his composition to the sense. If he is remembered for anything more tenaciously than for his Radical imagery it is for the ruggedness of his lines. The two situations are parallel. There is every indication that Donne had a musical ear, for he wrote several isolated passages of rare lyrical grace. As he subordinates (wisely or not) rythmical smoothness to sense, he subordinates graceful imagery to his passion for self expression. He could write admirable imagery that is not Radical and long passages of effective verse, as in *The Progress of the Soul,* without occasional metaphor at all. Yet it might be wished that for each category a single poet might be found representing it so thoroughly as Donne represents this. In the character of his thought and feeling the humanistic significance of this imagery lies revealed.

One of the best known of his figures will serve as a preliminary illustration of the category. Grosart speaks of

it as "the quaint but really magnificent image," and continues his criticism by quoting Coleridge on the same subject. "An admirable poem, which none but Donne could
have written. Nothing was ever more admirably made out
than the figure of the compass."

> Our two souls therefore, which are one,
>   Though I must go, endure not yet
> A breach, but an expansion,
>   Like gold to airy thinness beat.
>
> If they be two, they are two so
>   As stiff twin compasses are two;
> Thy soul, the fix'd foot, makes no show
>   To move, but doth if th' other do.
>
> And though it in the center sit,
>   Yet, when the other far doth roam,
> It leans, and harkens after it,
>   And grows erect as that comes home.
>
> So wilt thou be to me, who must,
>   Like th' other foot, obliquely run;
> Thy firmness makes my circle just,
>   And makes me end where I begun.
>   *Valediction Against Mourning*

The definition of this category can conveniently be arrived
at by contrasting this figure with illustrations from other
categories.

Four Expansive images are for various reasons of interest in this contrast. The selection of three of these from
Donne will support my observation that he by no means
confines himself to one form of imagery.

> Who vagrant transitory comets sees
>   Wonders because they're rare; but a new star
> Whose motion with the firmament agrees
>   Is miracle; for there no new things are.
>   *To the Countess of Huntingdon*

And now good-morrow to our waking souls.
The Good-Morrow

Thou art the proclamation; and I am
The trumpet at whose voice the people came.
II Anniversary

yet, wer't thou as far
As that vast shore wash't with the farthest sea,
I should venture for such merchandise.
Rom. and Jul. II, 2, 82

The discovery of a new star "where no new things are" is
a noble reference to the conception of intellectual progress
and the continuity of moral ideas. While the idea of the
heavens stimulates the imagination, a compass in general
does not. "Good-morrow" is the kernel of the second figure. The reference seems on first examination to be a
familiar one. When however one considers that here we
have the sum of all glad good-morrows, with thoughts of
friends who were seen anew, greetings to new suns and to
new worlds of hope begun, the full force of the idea appears. The requirement of Radical imagery is not that the
minor term in the figure shall be familiar but that it shall
be of little imaginative value. Here the general conception
of "good-morrow" is a highly stimulating one. The figure of the stars is sublime. That of "good-morrow" is
comprehensive. That of the trumpeter, the people and the
proclamation, though surprising, is dignified, brilliant,
noble and colorful. The picture is an engaging one. The
lines are, it will be recalled, the last in *The Second Anniversary*. The image from Shakespere, in spite of its reference to a subject which we have been taught to believe
unpoetic, is of the greatest scope and daring. We are to
imagine "that vast shore wash't by the farthest sea!"
All four figures then contrast with Radical metaphor.
The Radical image differs still more decisively from the

Exuberant. A single citation will illustrate the distinction. When Emilia recognizes Othello's crime she cries,

O gull, O dolt, as ignorant as dirt!

V, 2, 163

The relation is as vague as it is strong. Dirt is in fact no more ignorant than air, fire or water. There is no convention which holds dirt notoriously ignorant. Although there is enough suggestiveness to make the relation of dirt and ignorance metaphor, the real value of the figure is not in its nominal significance but in its implications. By this vigorous exclamation Emilia sums up in a single word all that her somewhat coarse mind conceives of Othello's tragic folly. The minor term in a Radical image is significant metaphorically only at a single, narrow point of contact. Elsewhere it is incongruous. Emilia's image has no single and just but narrow application. It is impressionistic. Emilia's figure is vulgar. The idea of the compass is presumably neutral. Radical metaphor is not to be thought of as coarse. Figures that are coarse are as a rule Violent, though the coarse and Exuberant figure from Othello is worthy of the supremely tragic scene where it so dramatically occurs.

All the five images contrasted with *A Valediction Against Mourning* may so far as their minor terms are concerned be looked upon unemotionally. It is possible to look on the stars without solemn thought. It is possible to take the trumpeter and his proclamation lightly, and to think meanly of an adventure for merchandise, even to "that vast shore wash't by the farthest sea." Dirt may be thought of without prejudice. It is difficult to recall the use of the word good-morrow in a general and a poetic sense by any writer beside Donne. Conversely a compass may possibly stir the poetic imagination. The invention of the first compass may be thought of as an august event in the history of mankind. Is then the distinction between essentially imaginative and unimaginative ideas a sound one ? Is everything in the imaginative world seen according to its context and has nothing there an intrinsic value ? Although in discussing the Radical image it would be quite convenient in this difficulty to take the context of figures into account, this seems hardly necessary. I shall assume as a basis for discussion that there is a practical working distinction between objects that are of great or mean imaginative worth, disregarding their metaphorical possibilities and viewing them intrinsically. We may assume that in ninety-nine cases of an hundred a compass carries no lively suggestions of beauty or truth. Until a poet has shown the way it is difficult to make poetic metaphor out of such an object. If the compass is to be regarded as a prosaic idea for the bulk of mankind, stars, an official trumpeter, an adventure to the vast and farthest shores, and the general conceptions of dirt and good-morrow may be assumed to be imaginatively pregnant.

The Radical image might be expressed geometrically as a cone. On one end is a point of no imaginative value in itself from which radiate lines of powerful suggestion. An Expansive or an Exuberant figure might be represented as a double cone pinched in the center with widely radiating lines on each side. The central fusion of these lines represents the metaphorical relation. Each term in an Expansive or Exuberant figure modifies the other. In the Radical image in poetic metaphor the minor term is a tool used for a high purpose, but without intrinsic beauty or fascination.

Dismissing the question of what Radical metaphor is not, we may now advance to a description of the category with further illustrations from Donne. The following image is of unusual interest from the standpoint of definition. The minor term is forcibly neutralized. If taken in any other than a literal-minded sense the figure would produce precisely the opposite of the desired effect.

> But as some serpent's poison hurteth not
> Except it be from the live serpent shot,
> So doth her virtue need her here to fit
> That unto us, she working more than it.
>
> *I Anniversary*

The thought of the passage is subtle, beautiful and just. The figure however must be understood in the most literal-minded fashion, or the meaning is destroyed. The influence of good women and the poison of snakes is in itself a strange pair of ideas.

Donne often uses imaginative conceptions in metaphor, treating them in such a fashion that they become Radical. Mountains, rivers and seas are considered not in a romantic but in an analytical manner.

> Nor are, although the river keep the name,
> Yesterday's waters and to-day's the same.
>
> *I Anniversary*

> Thus vent thy thoughts; abroad I'll study thee,
>   As he removes far off that great heights takes.
>   How great love is presence best trial makes,
> But absence tries how long this love will be.
>   To take a latitude
>   Sun, or stars are fittest viewed
>   At their brightest: but to conclude
> Of longitudes what other way have we
> But to mark when and where the dark eclipses be.
>
> *Valediction to his Book*

A great river or mountain may stimulate the imagination. The sun may be divine. When however they are considered from such minute and technical aspects as those of the natural scientist, the surveyor or the navigator they lose heavily in imaginative value. This river is far from Keats'

conception of waters in their task of ablution around
earth's human shores. The mountains and the stars of
Donne are far from equivalent to the patient star and
snow covered hills of the Romantic poet. Donne purposely
excludes the romantic suggestiveness of these ideas. Observing points of physical geography he relates them to
just and subtle observations on the psychology of love.
Such is the technique of the Radical image.

The definition of this figure then is simple. It remains
to consider its function and significance. A familiar
charge against the so-called "metaphysical" poets, of whom
Donne is always regarded as the first and usually as the
most eminent, is that they are ingenious to the extent of
insincerity. Passion, Johnson argues in his *Life of Cowley,*
does not express itself and is not to be felt in what is here
called the Radical figure. Johnson is chiefly the critic of
Cowley. That poet sowed the Radical figure profusely in
his lighter verse, as, for example, in his pleasant and ingenious lyrics to his Mistress, while using it less frequently
in his serious poems. The earnestness of the earlier poet
suffered in Johnson's hands from the levity of the younger.
If there is one quality for which all the more important
poetry of Donne stands, whether his theme is love, satire
or religion, it is an insistent and perhaps even inartistic
intensity of feeling. From his ardent intensity, not from
an itching to be a wit or from overconsciousness as an artist, came his rugged lines and Radical metaphors. His intensity belongs equally to his simpler emotions and to his
passion for analysis. With as much fervor as he loved,
hated and adored, he analyzed his heart in his lyrics and
elegies, society in his satires and epistles, and theology in
his religious poems and *Anniversaries.* He is everywhere
sincere, outspoken and self revealing. His strong passions demand intellectual expression. Analytical thought
is with him not a choice but a necessity. His brain is a

sleepless commentary on his heart. Direct statement struggles against the difficulties of analyzing a complex nature in vain. Hence the mind of the introspective poet is driven to figures of close analysis, which are as a rule Radical. Scholastic subtlety is revived in his verse. His images are motivated not by a desire for beauty nor by a quest for ideal forms nor even by a zest for imaginative activity, but by a desire for truth in matters perplexed by the emotions.

These statements may be supported by groups of citations. Here are illustrations from Donne of Radical figures in passages of undoubtedly high emotional pitch.

> Our hands were firmly cemented
>   By a fast balm, which thence did spring;
> Our eye-beams twisted, and did thread
>   Our eyes upon one double string.
>   *The Ecstacy*

> He which not knowing her sad history
> Should come to read the book of destiny,
> How fair and chaste, humble and high she had been,
> Much promised, much performed at not fifteen,
> And measuring future things by things before
> Should turn the leaf to read, and read no more,
> Would think that either destiny mistook
> Or that some leaves were torn out of the book.
>   . . . If after her
> Any should live which dare to good prefer,
> Every such person is her delegate
> T'accomplish that which should have been her fate.
>   *I Anniversary*

> Alas, hearts do not in eyes shine,
> Nor can you more judge women's thoughts by tears
> Than by her shadow what she wears.
>   *Twickenham Garden*

The emotional pitch of *The Ecstacy* is so intense that it

may be taken to strain the bounds of sympathy and intel-
ligibility. If by chance the images in the cited stanza fail
to attract us, their failure can only be ascribed to an over-
powerful emotion, never to ingenious trifling.

Consider with what art the following metaphors refine
upon the poet's thought.

> (on death)
> And think that but unbinding of a pack
> To take one precious thing, thy soul, from thence.
> *II Anniversary*
>
> She who in th' art of knowing heaven was grown
> Here upon earth to such perfection
> That she hath ever since to heaven she came
> In a far fairer print but read the same.
> *II Anniversary*
>
> To our bodies turn we then, that so
>   Weak men on love reveal'd may look;
> Love's mysteries in souls do grow,
>   But yet the body is his book.
> *The Ecstacy*
>
> 'Tis much this glass should be
> As all-confessing and through-shine as I;
>   'Tis more that it shows thee to thee
>   And clear reflects thee to thine eye.
> But all such rules love's magic can undo;
>   Here you see me and I am you.
> *On His Name Engraved in a Window*

It would be difficult to paraphrase the figure on death and
the packman. It illustrates the fine pregnancy that belongs to metaphorical expression. The meaning of the
saint reading in heaven a familiar book in a fairer print
is readily grasped but equally hard to explain in literal
language. The image is not merely illustrative; it has posi-
tively advanced the intellectual progress of the poem.
Similarly literal statement could only at great length, if

at all, reproduce the thought in the subtle stanza cited from *The Ecstacy.* The last line in the fourth citation is a masterful image in the "metaphysical" style. Psychology becomes poetry and engraves imperishable images on the memory.

Radical figures not only clarify obscure ideas but give a vivid rendering to familiar ones.

> As no one point nor dash,
> Which are but accessories to this name,
>   The showers and tempests can outwash,
>   So shall all times find me the same.
> You this entireness better may fulfill
>   Who have the pattern with you still.
> > *On His Name Engraved in a Window*

> This, as an amber drop enwraps a bee,
> Covering, discloses your quick soul, that we
> May in your through-shine face our hearts' thoughts see.
> > *To The Countess of Bedford*

> (Of the Countess and her daughter)
> Paired like two eyes, have equal motion so,
> Both but one means to see, one way to go.
> > *To The Countess of Bedford*

> Who makes the last a pattern for next year
>   Turns no new leaf but still the old things reads.
> Seen things he sees, heard things again doth hear,
>   And makes his life but like a pair of beads.
> > *To Sir Henry Goodyere*

This type of image, as might readily be inferred, is a common resort of the mystic. Driven from the possibility of literal statement, he still confronts a mystery which demands some measure of expression. Humility may force him to dispense with a bold attempt to comprehend the mystery through the highly sympathetic Expansive figure. Radical imagery is to some degree incongruous; and the mystic believes that between his noblest conception and the

object of his faith an incongruity is inevitable. He will
turn therefore to this unadorned and confessedly inade-
quate type of metaphor, perhaps finding in its seeming
precision a semblance of logical validity. Thus to the
medieval mystic the mystery of the Trinity is perceptibly
relieved by symbols from circles and triangles. Even the
greatest medieval poets have used these figures, believing
them not their own images, but instituted by God in the
creation of the world. The significance of geometric figures in Neoplatonic philosophy masked one of the most
mystical of sects with one of the most precise of the sciences. Donne in his mystical poetry uses many figures
from *"le géomètre enflammé."* Often both as skeptic and
·mystic he hesitates—and finds here the one available medium for expression. The humanistic significance of this
imagery he has himself expressed in his phrase, "a naked,
thinking heart." Elsewhere he shows his felicity in self
criticism :

> thou which lovest to be
> Subtle to plague thyself.
>
> *The Blossom.*

From such a man comes such imagery. It is not the greatest imagery in Donne. It is however most characteristic
of him. It is an essential medium of expression for one of
the most darkly fascinating personalities in Elizabethan
literature.

These citations from Shakespere illustrate the Radical
figure in passages of unusual emotional value. To recall
the emphasis upon the last line of the Fourth Act of *Troilus
and Cressida* I have cited the three tragic lines which precede it.

> O sir, to such as boasting show their scars
> A mock is due. Will you walk on, my lord?
> She was belov'd, she lov'd: she is, she doth:
> But still sweet love is food for fortune's tooth.
>
> *T. and C.* IV, 5, 290

And almost thence my nature is subdu'd
To what it works in, like the dyer's hand.
Pity me then and wish I were renew'd.

Son. 111

Go to your bosom;
Knock there, and ask your heart what it doth know
That's like my brother's fault.

M. for M. II, 2, 136

(of lust) a swallowed bait
On purpose laid to make the taker mad.

Son. 129

Upon the heat and flame of your distemper
Sprinkle cool patience.

Ham. III, 4, 123

Filial ingratitude!
Is it not as this mouth should tear his hand
For lifting food to 't.

Lear, III, 4, 14

A mote it is to trouble the mind's eye.

Ham. I, 1, 112

The Radical images in these familiar lines are less far-fetched than many of those in Donne, and are evidently the result of a more normal psychology. Like his Radical images, however, with the smallest of means they stimulate the imagination and move the heart.

Here are illustrations of somewhat difficult thought illuminated by the flash of the same metaphor.

Slaves are but nails to drive out one another.

Tourneur, *Revenger's Tragedy,* II, 103

Thou art thy mother's glass, and she in thee
Calls back the lovely April of her prime.

Son. 3

Fate's a spaniel,
We cannot beat it from us.

Webster, 49

> Heaven doth with us as we with torches do,
> Not light them for themselves.
>> *M. for M.* I, 1, 33

These are abstract ideas clarified by concrete and specific metaphor. In a striking image for the shipwreck in the Fourth Act of *A Winter's Tale* imagination passes from nature to nature. The zest of the figure rescues it from the neutral and prosaic comparison. By one of the most daring figures imaginable Shakespere in the compass of eight words clinches the picture.

> Sometimes to see 'em, and then not to see 'em; now the ship boring the moon with her main-mast, and anon swallowed with yeast and froth, as you'd thrust a cork into a hogshead.
>> *W. T.* III, 3, 91

This is hitting the metaphorical nail on the head.

After examining from Donne figures of emotional and intellectual value, those that make vivid relatively familiar ideas were illustrated. These have a similar effect.

> Things being worse begin to mend; the bee
> When he hath shot his sting into your hand
> May then play with your eyelid.
>> Webster, 85

> Every small thing draws a base mind to fear
> As adamant does iron.
>> Webster, 83

> Gilded pills.
>> Webster, 22

> Thy wrath like flaming wax hath spent itself.
>> Tourneur, *Revenger's Tragedy,* II, 51

> Sorrow makes her look like an oft dyed garment.
>> Ib. II, 94

> She carv'd thee for her seal, and meant thereby
> Thou shouldst print more, not let the copy die.
>> *Son.* 11

My mind is like to the asbeston-stone,
Which if it once be heat in flames of fire
Denieth to becomen cold again.
                    Greene, *Alphonsus,* 565

In the last two lists the citations from Webster and
Tourneur suggest that Radical imagery in an incisive form
is eminently dramatic. Few dramatists exceed these two
in this thrusting, rapier-like art. It invigorates and punc-
tuates their dialogue. Sometimes we may feel that this
metaphor is overworked, and that speeches bristle with
Radical images not thoroughly a part of the general conception. The dialogue of Shakespere stimulated as it is
by the same imagery, as for example in the scene between
Hamlet and his mother, remains smooth and retains an accumulative affect.

To conclude the description of the category so far as its
immediate content is concerned, the minor terms of the figures already cited may be reviewed. By this means the low
imaginative value of that term in Radical metaphor may be
observed. We have cited figures of Donne from a compass,
from scientific observations on the serpent's poison, on the
waters of a river, on the elevation of mountains and on the
determination of longitude; from glue, from a string, from
a damaged book, from a shadow, from a packman's bundle,
from a new edition of a book, from the psychology of reading and assimilation, from a name scratched on a window
pane, from a drop of amber that shuts in a bee, from the
resemblance of the left eye to the right and from the rereading of a page. The objects of the images from Shakespere have been: a tooth, a dyer's hand, fishbait, knocking
at a door, a sprinkling of water on flames, a mouth that
tears a hand, a mote that troubles an eye, a looking glass,
the serviceability of torches, a cork in an hogshead and a
seal. From Webster and Tourneur have been cited figures
from the driving out of nails, a spaniel, a bee without his

sting, a magnet, gilded pills, and an ill-dyed garment; finally from Greene comes a figure of a stone that retains heat. Through Radical imagery lines of unusual poetic merit arise from such unpromising and, it would seem, prosaic allusions.

In Donne and his followers and in the plays of Webster, Marston, Chapman, Tourneur and Shakespere, Radical metaphor reached its crest. In the more conservative Spenser it is scarcely to be found. The form flourished most generally where men and women eager to sound their own emotions and the emotions of one another soliloquized and conversed on the tragic stage. In the following generation Cowley in poetry and Thomas Fuller in prose best exemplify the form. No type was of course more discredited in English poetry of the eighteenth century. Beauty characterized the greater range of images open to the poets of the Romantic Revival. Radical figures seldom appear. Among the greater Victorians Browning alone uses the form frequently. Different as he is from Donne, who consumed himself inwardly and never impersonated another in verse or prose, the dramatically minded Browning often resembles Donne in the use of figures. The Elizabethan kept intellectual guard over his own emotions, Browning over the emotions of mankind. The same type of metaphor is naturally prominent in both. When the delicate taste of the Victorians in imagery yielded in popular favor to a more aggressive style, something of the daring of Elizabethan metaphor returned. The poems of George Meredith are an unusually condensed and interesting body of symbolic thought. He is indeed a bold adventurer in this type. Not only the thought but the imagery of Tourneur seems to return in such lines as these:

> But as you will, we'll sit contentedly
> And eat our pot of honey on the grave.
>
> *Modern Love,* 29

The larger number of Meredith's figures however are not Radical. The mind of Francis Thompson inclined him to the form, both as a mystic and a descriptive poet. The following image shows him in the latter capacity.

> At evening, when the lank and rigid trees
> To the mere forms of their sweet day-selves drying
> On heaven's blank leaf seem pressed and flattened.
>
> 247

The form has a recognized but not an important place in most contemporary verse. It belongs indeed rather to prose than to verse, for in poetry it requires skillful handling. Donne often accomplishes the transformation of the commonplace into the highly imaginative. Dante on the verge of his ultimate revelation transfigures the conception of a tailor cutting samples for a garment. Perhaps it is well that few minor poets should attempt an art in which only the masters have triumphed. In prose the Radical metaphor approaches the neutral comparison of science, becomes utilitarian, ceases to delight and is no longer poetic imagery. Although the Radical images cited in this chapter show in their minor terms no intrinsic imaginative value, they act as spurs to poetic thought. By an extraordinary feat of art they are made one with their imaginative content. Their emotional appeal is irresistible. They are not merely ingenious. They are not the exercises of wit. They are a part of the stuff of poetry. Of the Radical image of wit Swift is perhaps our foremost master. That however is matter for a later chapter. That the Radical image of poetic dignity occurs however in prose as well as in verse may be seen from the following words of Colet:

We seek not for victory in argument but for truth, which perchance may be elicited by the clash of argument, as sparks are made by the clashing of steel against steel.

1292

VI

THE INTENSIVE IMAGE

The Intensive image is one of high imaginative value in which clarity and concentration associate the minor term with pictorial art. Such metaphors are more often than others referred to as emblems or symbols. Few people would speak of these lines from *Romeo and Juliet* as symbolism.

> yet, wer't thou as far
> As that vast shore wash't with the farthest sea
> I should adventure for such merchandise.
>
> II, 2, 82

This is not Intensive but Expansive imagery. On the contrary the funereal cypress, which is an Intensive image, would very generally be called a symbol or an emblem. Let us consider these two figures in their relation to the fine arts. The cypress is a metaphor in ritual, in painting and in sculpture. Only a phenomenal achievement in painting or sculpture, however, could make the image in Romeo's lines intelligible. By highly suggestive technique, perhaps by personification, a Rodin might convey the idea of a merchant adventurer on a vast shore wash't by the farthest seas. Supposing such an extraordinary achievement, the pictorial art by which this idea is to be definitely related to a protest of affection is wanting. The second term of Romeo's figure is difficult to reproduce even literally, while the metaphorical idea seems definitely beyond the range of art. The poet is the expositor of his own images. He may point out to the reader a figurative relation here and there. He may draw upon scenes which no painter would venture to reproduce, and include the ideas of time and motion. The metaphor in the arts is restricted in space, gives at most only a metaphor of time and motion, speaks silently without an expositor and as a rule relies on the most limited means of suggestion. This distinction between literature and the fine arts does not rest alone on points of imagery. We may be admitted into the least thought that passes through the mind of an heroine in literature, while a painting, such as the Mona Lisa, may assure us rather of the artist's thoughtfulness than of the precise nature of his ideas. Frequently effective images in painting are not self explanatory. One must have a foreknowledge of the intent of the painter to appreciate the subtlety of his symbolism, which is metaphor only to the initiated. Restricted as the type of metaphor permissible in the fine arts may be, it is often found in literature as well, and especially in that Renaissance literature which flourished contemporaneously with the greatest schools of Western painting and by far our greatest schools of symbolic painting. Imagery in painting, sculpture, pageantry, heraldry and ritual contributed immensely to imagery in literature. This contribution I have called the Intensive metaphor. Beads for example are symbolical in religion. Spenser in eulogy of Chaucer adds personification to the emblem of the rosary. His master is

On Fame's eternal beadroll worthy to be filed.

Metaphorical personifications appear equally in the paintings of Botticelli and in the pages of Spenser. Figures personified by the artist and the poet are often grouped and often engaged in a performance of ceremony. By each the artificiality of art is stressed. These then are among the common characteristics of symbolism in the fine arts and the Intensive Metaphor.

Allegory is, of course, an uninterrupted string of metaphors some of which are recurrent. It is closely related to

Intensive imagery, for in all its more advanced forms its continuous symbolism is conducted, like that of painting, largely by means of emblem and personification, without an expositor. Generalizations in the thought naturally induce formalities in imagery. Our immediate concern is, in part, to study the character of the Intensive image in allegory, but not to observe the relation of the figures to the narrative as a whole. Much of the material for this chapter has, then, been drawn from allegorical poetry.

Since Intensive images are associated with painting, in Elizabethan literature they resemble the symbolic figures in Renaissance painting, clear in outline, conventional in subject and attractive in color and design. Their foremost qualities are clarity and concentration. Here is a bit of word painting typical of Spenser.

> And round about the same her yellow hair,
> Having through stirring loosed their wonted band,
> Like to a golden border did appear,
> Framed in goldsmith's forge with cunning hand.
>
> _F. Q._ IV, 6, 20

Thus in one of the most dramatic moments of _The Fairie Queene_ appeared the face of Britomart to Artegal. Although the figure is not strong in the subjective element, it well illustrates Spenser's adherence to the technique of Intensive imagery. It is impossible to think of this figure without thinking of the art of the Renaissance, the painter and the goldsmith. On the contrary the figure previously cited from _Romeo and Juliet_ is equally typical of Shakespere, and boldly transcends the possibilities of the pictorial arts. Shakespere's figure is distinctively literary. Spenser's figure confirms the sistership of the Muses. He who wishes to make symbols which the world will admire elsewhere than from the written page must imitate the art represented in Spenser. In this art the Latin peoples have excelled. Latin culture has at no time been more thor-

oughly assimilated by the English than during the lifetime of Shakespere. In the history of English literature
it is naturally to the Elizabethan age that we look for the
highest technical development of the Intensive metaphor.

By clarity and concentration is not meant a glaring light
or a restricted vision. The Intensive image will be clear
and compact. It may however have as delicate a sphere
of suggestion and illumination as the winter moon behind
a cloud. An illustration of simplicity and concentration
in a figure which still produces a romantic effect appears in
the concluding lines of this suggestive stanza from *The
Fairie Queene.*

> But roof and floor and walls were all of gold
> But overgrown with dust and old decay,
> And hid in darkness, that none could behold
> The hue thereof; for view of cheerful day
> Did never in that house itself display,
> But a faint shadow of uncertain light:
> Such as a lamp whose life doth fade away,
> Or as the moon clothed with cloudy night
> Does show to him that walks in fear and sad afright.
>
> II, 7, 29

A blinding effulgence characterizes the imagery of Marlowe. Spenser's Intensive figures have, around a contour
of the utmost precision, a subtle and delicate aureole of
suggestion.—The Intensive figure is in itself beautiful or
impressive. The Radical figure, it will be recalled, is derived from an idea of no account to the imagination. They
resemble one another however in thus deeply affecting the
imagination by the simplest means.

In spite of this requirement of concentration, it is possible that a landscape may be treated in a manner not inappropriate to the Intensive technique. High seas and the
expansive prairie will in poetic metaphor presumably suggest the superhuman or the sublime. There is however a

more humane art by which nature becomes proportionally less than man. Fields are painted in a minute design of brilliant colors. This may be observed in the landscape backgrounds seen over the shoulders of angels and saints in early paintings. This art is observable in Spenser. From the landscape in *King Lear* arise the most sublime images. Lear addresses the thunder and Edgar depicts the cliffs of Dover in Promethean metaphors. The tempest that rages in *Macbeth* is itself a metaphorical accompaniment of tragic crime. An artist who might well despair of painting these scenes on back-drop or canvas might find the following summer landscape from Spenser quite within his range. It is not an example of Intensive imagery, but in contrast with the familiar Shakesperian figures it is a good illustration of the Renaissance Intensive technique. The poet expresses in metaphor the relief which the Knights of Maidenhead receive from the victory of Britomart.

> Like as a summer's day when raging heat
> Doth turn the earth and boiled rivers dry,
> And all brute beasts forced to refrain fro' meat
> Do hunt the shade where shrouded they may lie,
> And missing it fain from themselves to fly;
> All travellers tormented are with pain;
> A watry cloud doth overcast the sky
> And poureth forth a sudden shower of rain
> That all the weary earth recomforteth again.
>
> *F. Q.* IV, 4, 47

Fineness of expression is as essential in the Intensive figure as in the execution of a low relief. Within its narrow bounds the degree of finish must be high. There is less impulsive strength in this than in the Expansive image, but more delicacy and more conscious art. Some poets conceive the world of their imagination in vast proportions. Immensity is an essential part in Milton's conception of heaven and hell. The legions of God and Satan are untold and the height and depth of their abodes unbounded. Some poets on the contrary do not emphasize magnitude. Dante for example gives to Purgatory precise and no very imposing dimensions. One is surprised not at how many but at how few people are met on the ascent. Colloquies are as private as a confessional. There are no synods in an imperial Pandemonium. In Spenser also there is little emphasis on number or proportion. This type of poetry is readily adapted to the Intensive metaphor. It may therefore be suggestive to note a few examples of the artistic diminutive in *The Fairie Queene*, remembering that all such instances are illustrations of a metaphorical principle.

A little lowly hermitage it was.

I, 1, 34

Arrived there the little house they fill.

I, 1, 35

And neigh thereto a little chapel stood.

VI, 5, 35

A little path that was both steep and long.

I, 11, 55

It was a chosen plot of fertile land
Amongst wild waves set like a little nest,
As if it had by Nature's cunning hand
Been nicely picked out from all the rest.

II, 6, 12

Upon a little hillock she was placed.

VI, 9, 8

And every leaf that shaketh with the least
Murmur of wind her terror hath increast.

III, 7, 1

Restless, recomfortless, with heart deep grieved,
Not suffering the least twinkling sleep to start
Into her eye, which th' heart mote have relieved.

V, 6, 24

With one sweet drop of sensual delight.

II, 6, 8,

At last him to a little door was brought. . . .
Betwixt them both was but a little stride
That did the house of Richess from Hellmouth divide.

II, 7, 24

In these lines appear a tiny hermitage, a tiny house, chapel and path, a little island set like a nest in the wide waves and a little hillock on which the Pastoral Queen is enthroned. The subjective figures are however the more interesting. Fear is so delicate that the least trembling of a leaf increases it. Britomart cannot suffer "the least twinkling sleep to start into her eye." "One sweet drop of sensual delight" is enough to pacify the anger of the sensitive pastoral humankind. Finally in this world of subtle discriminations the houses of Richess and Hellmouth are separated by no more than "a little stride." These citations illustrate the minuteness and delicacy in Spenser's world of dreams. At one pole the diminutive becomes a phase of the Decorative convention in light verse. At the other it becomes one of the aspects of the poignancy of Dante. Somewhere between these two extremes stands the manner of Spenser, but in his more serious passages much nearer to Dante.

In the above citations the last four only are fully subjective. These illustrate man, the others nature. Two more images will give the contrast of the Intensive figure under these two conditions. It is largely with the fully subjective figure that we shall henceforth be concerned. The first of these citations is but slightly, the second largely, subjective.

So wept Duessa until eventide
That shining lamps in Jove's high heaven were light.

F. Q. I, 5, 19

For soon as mastery comes sweet Love anon
Taketh his nimble wings and soon away is gone.
                                III, 1, 25

Before considering the particular forms and functions of
this imagery, we may consider its place in Elizabethan
thought. Two minor topics are suggestive. An examination of Elizabethan book-plates shows the relation of the
Intensive figure to popular contemporary art, and the
choruses of the early drama its power to embody the
popular abstractions of the age. Of special interest is a
plate from The First Part of *Hieronimo,* a play by Kyd,
published in 1609. On a fanciful plaque decorated in the
lower corners by small picks and shovels appears an oval
with the inscription on its border: "Thou shalt labor till
thou return to dust." Inside the oval is a picture of a
field with a laborer working in the foreground. Behind
him stands a basket. Beyond a fence which runs across
the back of the picture is a row of four houses, behind
them a steeple. A line of conventional clouds above a zone
of clear sky balances the darkened foreground of the field.
The central figure of the harvester is the embodiment of
daily toil, a secular Piers Plowman. Here is one of the
many crude but effective wood-cuts with symbolic significance which modestly decorate the title pages of the quar-
tos, but which are, nevertheless, indicative of a great age
in English poetry. Folios had as a rule much more elaborate designs. Their title pages alone repay a special
study from the standpoint of symbolism. The *Poly-Olbion*
has a magnificent design, reproduced in the publication of
the Spenser Society. One of the most celebrated is from
Raleigh's *History of the World.* On this page appeared
Jonson's epigram, describing the allegorical figures.

From death and dark oblivion, near the same,
   This mistress of man's life, grave History,
Raising the world to good and evil fame,
   Doth vindicate it to eternity.

Wise Providence would so; that nor the good
   Might be defrauded nor the great secured,
But both might know their ways were understood,
   When vice alike in time with virtue dured.
Which makes that, lighted by the beamy hand
   Of Truth that searcheth the most hidden springs,
And guided by Experience whose straight wand
   Doth mete, whose line doth sound the depth of things;
She cheerfully supporteth what she rears
   Assisted by no strengths but by her own,
Some note of which each varied pillar bears,
   By which as proper titles she is known,
Time's witness, herald of Antiquity,
   The light of Truth, and life of Memory.

Underwoods, XLII

The epigram is an elaboration of a sentence in Cicero. A noble work supports a stately title-page, interpreted by an inscription resembling a religious dedication. Another fine title-page is that of the *Novum Organum,* 1620, with a ship sailing between two pillars and the inscription *Multi pertransibunt & augebitur scientia.*

Before discussing the dramatic choruses a preliminary distinction between allegory, metaphorical personification and the direct technique is necessary to establish working definitions. By metaphorical personification is meant the expression of an abstract idea or of an object or aspect of nature by a self-explanatory human form. A possible extension might to be sure admit ostensibly literal figures which in fact exceed their literal value. Such metaphorical personifications however are subtle and disputable. A single illustration will suffice. The final lines in the Second Act of *King Lear* are spoken by the heartless Cornwall.

Shut up your doors, my lord; 'tis a wild night.
My Regan counsels well. Come out o' the storm.

The last sentence is so far raised into the universal that Cornwall may well be considered not a certain noble who shut out a certain deposed king, but the impersonation of the inhuman heart which shuts the doors of mercy on mankind. Shakespere has so far transcended the tragedy of a man, Lear, and succeeded in writing a symbolic tragedy of all the misery that man brings on man, that the dramatic characters pass into a new category of art, cease to be individuals and become complete symbols. Metaphor consists in the duality. We have an incident in the story of an old King left shelterless, and mankind who in a thousand ways banish one another from human sympathy. A similar use of the word storm in implied metaphor occurs in the last stanza of Keat's *The Eve of Saint Agnes*. The lines read:

> And they are gone: ay, ages long ago
> These lovers fled away into the storm.

The words, at least to the present writer, seem to contain much more than a merely literal significance. Life has in all ages, in Keat's tragic conception, been a storm buffeting the heart's desire. The lovers think themselves happy, but pass out into the storm. The bright hopes of imagination are beaten to earth as flowers in a tempest. Yet to pursue the definition of such elusive metaphors further, however powerful the form may be and however close it may lie to the essential problem of art itself, would exceed both the scope and ambition of my essay.

The idea of metaphorical personification confined to dumb show may be exemplified. Much that has often been called personification naturally does not come under this category. In the *Moralities* of the early sixteenth century Anger rages, Fear trembles, Sorrow weeps, and Pity prays. These figures represent abstractions. They are not metaphor, for they do not express anger, fear, sorrow or pity symbolically. These qualities are enacted to a superlative degree. A hint may be a metaphor. The raging of Anger is however no more allegorical than the indignation which Lear pours upon Goneril. The figures in the *Moralities* are not metaphorically related to the passions, but identified with them. Tom's anger against Dick is renamed Anger's wrath against Innocence. Suppose on the contrary figures denominated by abstract qualities but without descriptive costume or gesture to pass over a stage. Such figures would no more be metaphorical personifications than those from the *Moralities*. The case would be one of sign symbolism only, as "x" in algebra. This condition describes many of the formal personifications, so called, of eighteenth century poetry. Typical metaphorical personification is found in the scenes of pageantry in *The Fairie Queene*. Desire, Grief, Faith, Hope, Charity, Nature, Life and Death by costume, gesture and action reveal their identity with the utmost effectiveness.

Since this is a matter of comparative literature a few illustrations may be drawn from literature at large to exemplify the definition further. A metaphorical personification is one which to be known needs only to be seen, or, if one prefers the more penetrating phrase of Spenser, where "soul is form and doth the body make." Take Goethe's Mephistopheles. His various costumes and forms exquisitely express his ribaldry and his audacious conceit. The embodiment of an idea, this idea is legible in all his extraordinary aspects. His gestures are especially significant. A good example of the symbol of universality appears in his derisive laughter, the laughter not of one devil against a certain luckless doctor but of all the fiends at human aspiration. To illustrate further, the apostrophe of Lucretius to Nature is a subtle but powerful metaphorical personification. Although the goddess is nowhere described, we are compelled to visualize the divine being whose smile pacifies the raging of the seas, who terrifies the winds and clouds, bringing joy to bird and beast and laughter to mankind. On the other hand, to conclude with a modern instance, there is little metaphorical personification in the choral figures in Hardy's *The Dynasts.* The Spirit of the Pities, The Spirit of the Ironies, The Spirit Sinister and The Spirit of the Years are known only as Voices, like those which Caliban heard on the Magic Island. It might be urged that the Spirits are instances of the universal symbolism illustrated from *King Lear.* There is in the case of Cornwall however a man of flesh and blood, an ancient Duke of Britain, sufficiently tangible and distinct when contrasted with the abstract conception of heartlessness to make a plausible metaphor. Hardy's Spirits however are only a literal and philosophical comment on mankind. A metaphor cannot be made of a single term.

The late sixteenth century drama affords many illustrations of metaphorical personification, shows the relation of the Intensive image to allegory, and indicates the native genius of the Elizabethans for emblematic thought. Six representative plays may be considered, ranging from Sackville and Norton's *Gorboduc* written in 1560 to Dekker's *Old Fortunatus* as acted in 1599. Personification appears in *Gorboduc* in the form of dumb-show. Spectacles introduce the five acts of the play. In the First Act the theme is announced. The play is designed to show the necessity of a united England under the newly enthroned Elizabeth. To symbolize this idea the players present the classical and familiar story of sticks that may be broken separately but not in a bundle. The introduction to Act Two also contains a political allusion. A just counselor offers a king a cup of good counsel, which he refuses. Then a flattering counselor offers him a cup of treacherous counsel, which he accepts. After draining the cup he is killed by the poison. Death is symbolized in Act Three by

a pageant of mourners.   In Act Four the Furies are the
symbols of wrath descending upon Britain.   In Act Five
appear the symbols of war and battle.   These scenes are
typical of the dumb-shows which played so important a
part on the early Elizabethan stage.

The Rare Triumphs of Love and Fortune is an anonymous play published in 1581.   The figures in personification are the gods of Olympus.   Love and Fortune are
fitted with appropriate emblems, play a considerable part
in the action, and with much brilliant and metaphorical
appeal to the eye contribute some moral dignity to the
scene.

The Three Lords and Three Ladies of London, published
in 1590 and written by Robert Wilson, is for the most part
a thoroughgoing allegory.   The climax however may be
viewed as an independent scene.   Here three Spanish
Lords, Policy, Pomp and Pleasure, in love with three English ladies, Love, Lucre and Conscience, challenge, through
their three pages, three lords and defenders of England.
The old form of allegory takes fire in representing one of
the most dramatic events in English history.   "The gov-
ernment of Spain is tyranny!" declares the English dramatist.   The overthrow of the Armada is represented by a
fencing contest as formal as Japanese symbolical dancing.
This play, then, shows the celebration of a great national
victory in sixteenth century England.   A contrast im-
mediately occurs with ceremonies in London for the victory
of 1918.   In these matters modern England must, I think,
confess inferiority.   Battles corresponding to those which
were of necessity symbolically represented on the Elizabethan stage may now to be sure be seen at the cinema.
For the greater artistic task, the effective embodiment of
abstract ideas in ceremony, one may well turn to the minor
relics of the old literature.

Not only in plays but in pageants and ballads the vic-

tory over Spain was celebrated with metaphorical personification. The opening lines of a song by Thomas Deloney
reflect credit both on the poet who composed and on the
populace which sang them.

> Noble England,
>   Fall down upon thy knee,
> And praise thy God with thankful heart,
>   Which still maintaineth thee!

468

Summer's Last Will and Testament by Thomas Nash is
neither masque, vaudeville, strict allegory nor pageant.
In this charming medley the author is constantly calling
attention to the appearance of his symbolical characters.
It is therefore of interest as a source for metaphorical
personifications. Here is one stage direction.

Enter Bacchus riding upon an ass trapt in ivy, himself
dressed in ivy leaves, and a garland of grapes on his head, his
companions having all jacks in their hands and ivy garlands
on their heads; they come in singing.

Vol. IV, 264

In the first address of Summer are these pleasant and
highly artificial lines (as given in the reading adopted by
Dodsley).

> Summer I am; I am not what I was;
> Harvest and age have whitened my green head.

Some of the plays offer little information on the appearance of the personified figures, but give a strong stimulus
to the visualizing imagination. It is clear that spectacle
and allegory are intimately associated. Such is evidently
the case in this chorus from *The Tragedy of Soliman and
Perseda,* by Thomas Kyd.

Fortune	I gave Erastus woe and misery
	Amidst his greatest joy and jollity.
Love	But I, that have power in earth and heaven above,
	Stung them both with never failing love.
Death	But I bereft them both of love and life.
Love	Of life but not of love! For even in death
	Their souls are knit though bodies be disjoined.
	Thou dids't but wound their flesh; their minds are free!
	Their bodies buried, yet they honor me!
Death	Hence foolish Fortune and thou wanton Love!
	Your deeds are trifles, mine of consequence.
Fortune	I give worlds happiness and woes increase.
Love	By joining persons I increase the world.
Death	By wasting all I conquer all the world.

The reader pauses to think how such figures would appear.

One of the most successful of the plays uniting personification with the direct manner is Dekker's *Old Fortunatus,* as presented in 1599. Fancy and charm in this play may cause the real strength of the symbolical passages to be overlooked. There are here for simple people serious ideas which one may easily neglect through admiration of the poet's facility. Dekker himself is not eminent as a philosopher, but he is representative of an eminently reflective age. Here are two of his principal stage directions, in which his metaphorical personifications appear:

Enter a Shepherd, a Carter, a Tailor and a Monk, all crowned; a Nymph with a globe, another with Fortune's wheel; then Fortune. After her four kings with broken crowns and scepters, chained in silver gyves and led by her. The foremost comes out singing. Fortune takes her chair; as the kings are lying at her feet she treads on them as she ascends her seat.

I, 1

A Forest in Cyprus

Music sounds. Enter Vice with a gilded face and horns on her head, her garments long, painted before with silver half moons, increasing by little and little till they come to the full. In the midst of them written in capital letters is, " *crescet eundo.*" Her garments are painted behind with fools' faces and devils' heads, and underneath it in the midst is written, " ha, ha, ha." She and others wearing gilded vizards, and attired like devils, bring out a fair tree of gold with apples on it.

After her comes Virtue with a coxcomb on her head, her attire all in white before, while about the middle is written, " *sibi sapit.*" Her attire behind is painted with crowns and laurel garlands stuck full with stars, held by hands thrust out of bright clouds, and among them is written, " *dominabitur astris.*" She and other nymphs, all in white with coxcombs on their heads, bring a tree with green and withered leaves mingled together and with little fruit on it.

After her comes Fortune, with one nymph bearing her wheel, another her globe, and the last, the Priest.

The priest after a few lines sings the following song.

> Virtue's branches wither, Virtue pines,
> > O pity, pity and alack the time!
> Vice doth flourish, Vice in glory shines,
> > Her gilded boughs above the cedar climb.
> Vice hath golden cheeks. O pity, pity,
> > She in every land doth merchandise.
> Virtue is exiled from every city;
> > Virtue is a fool, Vice only wise.
> O pity, pity, Virtue weeping dies!
> > Vice laughs to see her faint—alack the time!
> This sinks; with painted wings the other flies;
> > Alack that best should fall and bad should climb!

An elaborate pantomime may of course be supposed to have been conducted following the suggestions in this song. The expression by means of metaphorical personification must surely have been effective. Far-fetched as the comparison from some standpoints may be, in the general scheme of composition few English plays come closer to Hardy's grim tragedy of a continent than Dekker's charming and naïve entertainment acted before Queen Elizabeth.

Something of the popular significance of the Intensive
Metaphor in Elizabethan thought has been seen from wood
cuts and from the symbolical scenes in the early drama.
The simplest form of the Intensive image is the emblem.
Many personified figures in medieval sculpture and paint-
ing have emblems in their hands or on their garments.
Such also are the half moons on the robe of Vice and the
laurels and stars on the robe of Virtue in *Old Fortunatus*.
The grapes and ivy that decorate Bacchus and his train in
Summer's Last Will and Testament are likewise emblems.
To place an emblem in the hand of a personified figure is
the easiest means of suggesting its intention. The conventionality of medieval drawing and sculpture contributed to
the demand for emblems. By this means the figures of
saints that looked much alike might readily be identified.
Many of these emblems were metaphorical. The vogue of
Whitney and the later Emblem-books evinces their per-
sistence and popularity. Although heraldic emblems
played an important part in Elizabethan poetry, they seldom appeared more effectively than in the courtly verses
of Dunbar, which treat long familiar ideas in the full spirit
of the new age.

> Then callet she all flowris that grew in field,
>   Discerning all their fashions and affairs;
> Upon the awful Thistle she behild,
>   And saw him kepit with a bush of speiris;
>   Conced'ring him so able for the weiris
> A radius crown of rubeis she him gaef
> And said, " In field go forth and fend thyself." . . .
> Then to the Rose she turnit her visage . . .
> A costly crown with clarified stonis bright
>   This comely queen did on her head encloiss,
> Which all the land illumined of the light,
>   Wherefore me thought all flowris did rejoiss,
>   Crying at once, " Hail be thou richist Roiss!
> Hail, herbis empress, hail, freshest queen of flowris,
> To thee be glory and honor at all houris! "
>
>   *The Thistle and the Rose*

And first the Lion, greatest of degree
 Was callit there, and he most fair to seen
 With a full hardy countenance and kene
 Before dame Nature came. . . .
On field of gold he stood full michtely,
With fleur de lyce circulet lustely.
       The Thistle and the Rose

The emblem of the flower, an imperishable tradition in the guild of poets, serves equally in the symbolism of love and death and admits a remarkable number of variations. The tradition can best be discussed where representative figure are in view.

Soon after them, all dauncing in a row,
The lovely virgins came with girlands dight,
As fresh as flowers in meadows green do grow
When morning dew upon their leaves doth light.
    F. Q. I, 12, 6

The flower that's like thy face, pale primrose, nor
The azur'd harebell, like thy veins, no, nor
The leaf of eglantine, whom not to slander
Outsweet'ned not thy breath.
    Cym. IV, 2, 221

This bud of love, by summer's ripening breath,
May prove a beauteous flower when next we meet.
    Rom. and Jul. II, 2, 121

   See how she 'gins to blow
Into life's flower again.
    Per. III, 2, 95

This carol they began that hour,
 With a hey, and a ho, and a hey nonino,
How that a life is but a flower
 In the spring time!
    A. Y. L. I. V, 3, 28

I sent thee late a rosy wreath. . . .
    Jonson, 683

A chamber deaf to noise and blind to light;
A rosy garland and a weary head.
Astrophel and Stella, 39

Nay, better learn of them that learned be
And han be watered at the Muses' well;
The kindly dew drops from the higher tree,
And wets the little plants that lowly dwell.
Sp. *S. C.* XI, 29

The fairest flower our girlond all among
Is faded quite and into dust ygo.
Sp. *S. C.* XI, 75

The Muses that were wont green bays to wear
Now bringen bitter elder branches sere.
Sp. *S. C.* XI, 146

There's rosemary, that's for remembrance; pray, love,
remember; and there is pansies, that's for thoughts.
Ham. IV, 5, 175

Beauty is but a flower
Which wrinkles will devour;
Brightness falls from the air,
Queens have died young and fair.
Dust hath closed Helen's eye.
Nash, *Summer's Last Will and Testament*

These images have since the writers of the Greek anthology
been in the constant possession of the guild of poets.
Thousands of artists have accepted the task of perfecting
them. Elizabethan sonnet writers work anew on figures
long deposited in the common store. The old stocks are
continually putting forth new shoots. Consider for example the varieties through which the flower image passes
in the preceding citations. The first is an expression of
joy; the second is a bit of delicate description; the third is
a metaphor of love's growth; the fourth figures a resuscita-
tion; the fifth symbolizes life, joy and death; in the sixth

a wreath is a relic in love's religion; in the seventh a garland is an emblem of idleness; the eighth is a metaphor of humility; and the four remaining citations, highly differentiated, render the thought of death pitiful, solemn, tender and august. These are a few of the flowers which belong upon one unfading garland which the poets of all ages are weaving for the bliss and bitterness of life.

It is typical of Shakespere to give only the hint of a personification, while the figures of Spenser are elaborately painted. Of the latter form, which alone belongs to Intensive imagery, Spenser is beyond doubt the first master in Elizabethan poetry. Thoroughly metaphorical and emotional, his personifications contrast strongly both with the formalisms of later poetry and the dull feminising of abstract ideas in much medieval verse. Many of Spenser's figures show an extraordinary intensity of feeling and impressively embody his ideas. His personifications of Desire and Grief illustrate more especially this intensity; those of Faith, Hope and Charity, showing both his intensity and ideas, are of special interest in their relation to painting; those of Nature, Life and Death clothe no inconsiderable philosophy in a magnificent garment of poetic imagination.

> (*Desire*)
> His garment was disguised every vain
> And his embroidered bonnet set awry;
> Twixt both his hands few sparks he close did strain
> Which still he blew and kindled busily,
> That soon they life conceived, and forth in flames did fly.
>
> *F. Q.* III, 12, 9

> Grief all in sable sorrowfully clad,
> Down hanging his dull head with heavy cheer,
> Yet inly being more than seeming sad.
> A pair of pincers in his hand he had
> With which he pinced people to the heart,
> That from thenceforth a wretched life they led.
>
> III, 12, 16

(*Fidelia*)

She was arrayed all in lily white,
And in her right hand bore a cup of gold
With wine and water filled up to the hight,
In which a serpent did himself enfold,
That horror made to all that did behold;
But she no whit did change her constant mood.
And in her other hand she fast did hold
A book, that was both signed and sealed with blood,
Wherein dark things were writ, hard to be understood.

Her younger sister that Speranza hight
Was all in blue that her beseemed well;
Not all so cheerful seemed she of sight
As was her sister; whether dread did dwell
Or anguish in her heart is hard to tell.
Upon her arm a silver anchor lay
Whereon she leaned ever as befell;
And ever up to heaven, as she did pray,
Her steadfast eyes were bent, ne swerved other way.

(*Charissa*)

She was a woman in her freshest age,
Of wondrous beauty and of bounty rare,
With goodly grace and comely personage,
That was on earth not easy to compare;
Full of great love, but Cupid's wanton snare
As hell she hated; chaste in work and will;
Her neck and breasts were ever open bare
That aye thereof her babes might suck their fill;
The rest was all in yellow robes arrayed still.

A multitude of babes about her hung
Playing their sports that joyed her to behold,
Whom still she fed whilst they were weak and young,
But thrust them forth still as they waxed old;
And on her head she wore a tyre of gold
Adorned with gems and owches wondrous fair,
Whose passing price uneath was to be told;
And by her side there sat a gentle pair
Of turtle doves, she sitting in an ivory chair.

I, 10, 13–31

Then forth issued great Goddess, great Dame Nature,
With goodly port and gracious majesty,
Being far greater and more tall of stature
Than any of the gods or powers on high.
Yet certes by her face and physnomy
Whether she man or woman inly were
That could not any creature well descry;
For with a veil that wimpled everywhere
Her head and face was hid that mote to none appear.

That, some do say, was so by skill devised
To hide the terror of her uncouth hue
From mortal eyes that should be sore agrized,
For that her face did like a Lion shew
That eye of wight could not endure the view;
But others tell that it so beauteous was
And round about such beams of splendor threw
That it the sun a thousand times did pass,
Ne could be seen but like an image in a glass.

That well may seemen true. For well I ween
That this same day when she on Arlo sat
Her garment was so bright and wondrous sheen
That my frail wit cannot devise of what
It to compare nor find like stuff to that.
As those three sacred saints, though else most wise,
Yet on mount Thabor quite their wits forgat,
When they their glorious Lord in strange disguise
Transfigured saw; his garments so did daze their eyes.

VII, 7, 5

And after all came Life and lastly Death,
Death with a grim and grizly visage seen;
Yet is he naught but parting of the breath
Ne ought to see, but like a shade to ween,
Unbodied, unsouled, unheard, unseen;
But Life was like a fair young lusty boy
Such as they fain Dan Cupid to have been,
Full of delightful health and lively joy,
Deckt all with flowers, and wings of gold fit to employ.

VII, 7, 46

The allegorical conceptions of Desire and Grief are indeed poignant. Fidelia, Speranza and Charissa are as moving and delightful as good theological pictures. In the radiant figure of Nature sitting in the sunrise upon her throne on Arlo hill we have a union of intellect and mysterious splendor, reflection and poetic imagination. In the last cited stanza Spenser gives concise and artistic expression to his view of the world. Life is a pursuit of the happiness afforded by Nature, and Death a spectral unreality. It is altogether characteristic of the poet of *The Fairie Queene* to embody a forward looking philosophy in the beauty of medieval allegorical devices. Spenser maintained the effective medieval metaphorical technique in perfect harmony with the ideals of the Renaissance. As the content of medieval thought became increasingly unpalatable, the glass which contained it was by later poets cast impatiently against the wall.

Each of these citations from Spenser is extended through several lines. Most of his finest personifications are developed in this leisurely fashion. Ah, the divine leisure of that Fairie masterpiece! Shakespere shows the incisive, dramatic manner. This for example is a passing phrase in *Cymbelene:*

> yet reverence,
> That angel of the world.

IV, 2, 247

The following personifications are notably metaphorical at only a single point. This manner is representative of Shakespere. In the first image the chief figurative element is nakedness; in the second craftsmanship; in the third a noiseless footstep; in the fourth a silver hand; in the fifth a rugged one; in the sixth the easy poise of a lord upon his throne; and in the last the enthronement of a queen.

Therefore they always smoothly seem to smile,
That we likewise should mild and gentle be;
And also naked are, that without guile
Of false dissemblance all them plain may see,
Simple and true, from covert malice free.

F. Q. VI, 10, 24

'Tis beauty truely blent, whose red and white
Nature's own sweet and cunning hand laid on.

T. N. I, 5, 258

For we are old, and on our quicks't degrees
The inaudible and noiseless foot of Time
Steals ere we can effect them.

All's Well, V, 3, 40

You, Lord Archbishop,
Whose see is by a civil peace maintain'd,
Whose beard the silver hand of peace hath touch'd.

II Hen. IV, IV, 1, 41

Then let not winter's ragged hand deface
In thee thy summer, ere thou be distilled.

Son. 6

My bosom's lord sits lightly on his throne.

Rom. and Jul. V, 1, 3

Thy countenance as if Science held her seat
Between the circled arches of thy brows.

Greene, *Friar Bacon,* 1213

The two images which follow illustrate further possibilities of the form. I have cited the first for its heroic vigor, the second for its familiarity and ease.

O Piso, think,
Think on that day when in the Parthian fields
Thou criedst to th' flying legions to turn
And look Death in the face. He was not grim
But fair and lovely when he came in arms.

The Tragedy of Nero

Last of all, thou lady of clowns and carters, schoolmistress of fools and wiseacres, thou homely but harmless Rusticity, Oh breath thy dull and dunstical spirit into our Gander's quill! Crown me thy poet, not with a garland of bays, Oh no, the number of those that steal the lauret is too monstrous already, but swaddle thou my brows with thy unhandsome boughs, which like Autumn's rotten hair hang dangling over thy dusty eyelids. Help me, thou midwife of unmannerliness, to be delivered of this embryon that lies tumbling in my brain. Direct me in this hard and dangerous voyage, that being safely arrived on the desired shore I may build up alters to thy unmatchable rudeness.

Dekker, *Cull's Hornbook, Introduction*

Personification, which was a part of the web and woof of men's thought during the lifetime of Shakespere, became in the eighteenth century in large measure a monopoly of the poets. A type of metaphorical expression which came with equal ease to the author of *The Tragedy of Nero* and to Dekker, which was equally appropriate to minds in highly classical or in informal dress, became largely restricted to a grandiloquent manner. Milton maintains the warmth of the Elizabethan personifications without their exuberance, and possesses the dignity of the best eighteenth century personifications without their starched formality. His figures hold a middle station, at once lively and flexible, elevated and august. Here for example are two metaphorical personifications which are classical in their formality but which breathe and glow with the warmth and invention of the earlier manner.

> But he, her fears to cease,
> Sent down the meek-eyed Peace;
> She crowned with olive green came softly sliding
> Down through the turning sphere
> His ready harbinger,
> With turtle wings the amorous clouds dividing;
> And waving wide her myrtle wand
> She strikes a universal peace through sea and land.
>
> *Hymn to the Nativity*

Thus passed the night so foul, till morning fair
Came forth with Pilgrim steps in amice grey;
Who with her radiant finger stilled the roar
Of thunder, chased the clouds, and laid the winds.
                    Par. Reg. IV, 426

Leaving temporarily those personifications which symbolize abstract ideas, we may consider a few of the Elizabethan personifications of the aspects of nature. Here are
two figures of the setting sun, two images of the sun under
a cloud, four metaphors of morning, one of the moon and
one of the stars, in all ten pieces taken from the purse of
poetry.

The glorious sun went blushing to his bed.
                    Drayton, *Son.* 25

How oft have I descending Titan seen
        His burning locks couch in the sea queen's lap,
        And beautious Thetis his red body wrap
In watery robes, as he her lord had been.
                    Greene, *Menaphon*

And in a sable mantle of disgrace
Set him that is yclept bright heaven's eye.
                    Greene, *Never Too Late*

Black is the beauty of the brightest day,
The golden ball of heaven's eternal fire
That danced with glory on the silver waves
Now wants the fuel that enflamed his beams,
And all with faintness and for foul disgrace
He binds his temples with a frowning cloud.
                    Marlowe, *II, Tamb.* I, 4, 1

See how the morning smiles
On her bright eastern hill,
And with soft steps beguiles
Them that lie slumbering still.
                    Campion, *Airs,* Book II

Modest as morning when she coldly eyes
The youthful Phoebus.

T. and C. I, 3, 229

But look, the morn in russet mantle clad
Walks o'er the dew of yon high eastern hill.

Ham. I, ι, 166

Look, love, what envious streaks
Do lace the severing clouds in yonder east!
Night's candles are burnt out, and jocund day
Stands tiptoe on the misty mountain tops.

Rom. and Jul. III, 5, 8

Wherewith kind Cynthia in the heaven that shined,
Her nightly veil resigned
And her fair face disclosed.

England's Helicon, 206

Night like a masque has entered heaven's high hall
With thousand torches ushering the way.

Marston, *The Insatiate Countess,* V

The personifications cited from Drayton, Greene and Marlowe are the "brave" conventions for which early Elizabethan verse was celebrated. The figures from Shakespere are less bold, less sensuous, subtler and more subjective.

Frequently personified figures are imagined in a group. This type most strongly suggests the pictorial arts, and might well be illustrated not only from poetry but from the records of the coronation pageants of Henry VIII and Queen Elizabeth and of the festivals of the Lord Mayor. These two stanzas show Spenser's favorite pictorial technique of pairing his figures—a device familiar to Dante, Petrarch, Boccaccio and Chaucer—and the accumulative effect which Spenser obtained.

And next to her sat goodly Shamefastness,
Ne ever durst her eyes from ground uprear,
Ne ever once did look up from her desse,
As if some blame of evil she did fear;
That in her cheeks made roses oft appear.
And her against sweet Cheerfulness was placed,
Whose eyes like twinkling stars in evening clear
Were dekt with smiles that all sad humors chased,
And darted forth delights the which her goodly graced.

And next to her sat sober Modesty,
Holding her hand upon her gentle heart;
And her against sat comely Courtesy
That unto every person knew her part;
And her before was seated overthwart
Soft Silence and submiss Obedience,
Both linked together never to dispart,
Both gifts of God, not gotten but from thence,
Both girlonds of his saints against their foes offence.

F. Q. IV, 10, 50

In his dedicatory Sonnet to *The Fairie Queene* Sir Walter Raleigh conceived one of the noblest of Elizabethan group personifications, as it is one of the most elaborate. In the picture are included the Fairie Queene and the Vestal Graces attendant upon the tomb of Laura. The passage comes to its culmination in a vision of Oblivion. Raleigh has wandered in a dream to the grave of Petrarch's beloved:

and passing by that way
To see that buried dust of living fame
Whose tomb fair Love and fairer Virtue kept,
All suddenly I saw the Fairie Queene,
At whose approach the soul of Petrarch wept.
And from thenceforth those graces were not seen;
For they this Queen attended. In whose stead
Oblivion laid him down on Laura's hearse.

Allied to the topic of group personification is that of ceremony. Ceremony is measured metaphorical action. It is formal and intense dramatic allegory. Shakespere in his Twenty-Third Sonnet speaks of ''The perfect ceremony of love's rite.'' Much more elaborate is the sonnet in the Masque Scene at the house of Capulet.

Rom.   If I profane with my unworthiest hand
                This holy shrine, the gentle fine is this:
          My lips, two blushing pilgrims, ready stand
                To smooth their rough touch with a tender kiss.
Jul.   Good pilgrim, you do wrong your hand too much,
                Which mannerly devotion shows in this;
          For saints have hands that pilgrims' hands do touch
                And palm to palm is holy palmers' kiss.
Rom.   Have not saints lips, and holy palmers too?
Jul.   Ay, pilgrim, lips that they must use for prayer.
Rom.   O, then, dear saint, let lips do what hands do;
          They pray, grant thou, lest faith turn to despair.
Jul.   Saints do not move, though grant for prayer's sake.
Rom.   Then move not, while my prayer's effect I take.

While the ceremony of drama may include that of pantomime, it may exceed it in design by the addition of a verse pattern. Measured and formal action enters into the definition of ceremony. This is enhanced by the language of highly artificial verse spoken by Romeo.

All critics of Elizabethan literature have agreed to admire the closing sonnet in Michael Drayton's *Idea*. The last six lines of this poem contain a crowning example of ritualistic, group, metaphorical personification, with which our citations of the Intensive image in Elizabethan poetry may fittingly close. The sonnet is introduced with the Intensive emblems of the parting kiss and the shaking of hands after a lover's quarrel. The conclusion is as follows.

Now at the last gasp of Love's latest breath,
When his pulse failing Passion speechless lies,
When Faith is kneeling by his bed of Death
And Innocence is closing up his eyes:
> Now if thou would'st, when all have given him over,
> From Death to Life thou mights't him yet recover.

Finally, no Elizabethan lyric better sustains ritualistic imagery than Royden's heart-wrung elegy on his friend Sidney.

After the Age of Shakespere images of ritual passed all too quickly from the pages of English poetry. The rising Puritanism was a hostile force. The imagery of poetry suffered with that of the churches. Ritualistic figures were far from the temper of lovers in the period of the Restoration and during the lifetime of Pope. Yet, to cite a single poet, the passing glow of the earlier imagery casts a ray over some verses by Bishop King. These endure comparison with the lines of Drayton on a similar theme. King's lyric is also a record of renunciation and parting.

Fold back our arms, take home our fruitless loves,
That must new fortunes try, like turtle doves
Dislodged from their haunts. We must in tears
Unwind a love knit up in many years.
In this last kiss I here surrender thee
Back to thyself; so, thou again art free.
Thou in another, sad as that, resend
The truest heart that Lover ere did lend.
The Surrender

There is no need to discuss in detail the guild images in *Lycidas*. These are perhaps the finest examples in our language of the secular ritual of poetry. The figure of ceremony appears in every section, and is essential in the conception and construction of the poem. The spirit of

ritual is seen in the laurels and brown myrtles shaken over
the grave, in the figure of the sacred well, in the account of
the ordered pastoral day, in the ceremony of the mourning
year and in the pastoral lament, in the Orphic tragedy, in
the sporting of Panope and her sisters, in the procession in
which walk Camus and Saint Peter, in the ritual of flowers,
in the rythmic movements of the "sweet societies" of
heaven and in the formal departure of the singer himself.
Ceremony is a measured metaphorical action.   Here is its
apotheosis.

VII

THE EXPANSIVE IMAGE

The Expansive image is one in which each term opens a wide vista to the imagination and one in which each term is strongly modified by the other. Since both of its parts have a high imaginative value and mutually assist one another without depreciation, it is sharply distinguished from the Decorative image. It differs from the Sunken figure in that its terms are fully visualized or realized. It differs from the Violent metaphor in three respects; the intellectual and emotional elements are not lost in the sensational; even if examined with fixed attention the relation is appropriate; and there is a delicate modification to particular instances. It differs from the Radical category since in that figure one term is of low imaginative value and while modifying its partner remains itself unmodified. It is distinguished from the Intensive image chiefly in that its minor term offers a wide scope to the imagination. The Intensive figure is seen in emblems and personifications, while the Expansive metaphor casts one extended experience against another, with a well developed conception of time or action in the minor term. The minor terms of the Intensive image are fixed, the imagination without radically modifying these terms receiving from them a powerful stream of suggestion. In the Expansive figure the minor term itself is subject to profound modification. This may readily be seen by contrasting an emblem in religion, such as the lily, with the image already cited from *Romeo and Juliet*.

> wer't thou as far
> As that vast shore wash't by the farthest sea
> I should adventure for such merchandise.

The mind is led by the lily, a symbol of surprising beauty and simplicity, to the conceptions of chastity and immortality. Whatever excursions into a heaven the imagination may take, the lily itself remains unchanged. The angels bear the unalterable symbol in their hands. On the contrary Romeo's conception of the vast, perilous and uttermost shore may undergo endless modifications. Every fresh suggestion of obstacles to love makes the cliffs more terrible and obscure, and every darkening shadow that falls over the cliffs and sea suggests new obstacles to passion. The minor term in Romeo's image is scarcely less modified than the major. In place of the constant symbol of the lily we have the creative imagination working in unceasing change. Finally the Expansive figure is distinguished from the Exuberant. In the former the two terms not only modify each other but show a specific cause for their dependence, while in the latter the two terms are associated only by some vague confusion of the senses or by the opposition of splendor to splendor or beauty to beauty. Exuberant metaphor, typical of Marlowe, is often hyperbolical. Its extreme impressionism removes it farthest from the neutral comparison. The Expansive category however fulfills to the highest degree that standard for metaphor which concerns the mutual modification of its terms. Beauty, vigor, terror, a surcharged imagination, a lively fancy and a contemplative mind all find expression in the form. It is at once the language of strong passion and original meditation, of Othello and Francis Bacon. The first part of this chapter will deal with images of emotion, the second with figures of fancy, and the remainder with metaphors of contemplation. The representative Elizabethan held in equal regard a strong emotionalism and an imaginative inquiry into life. Expansive imagery flourishes in such a culture.

Obviously those figures containing abstract ideas in the

minor term cannot belong to Intensive imagery. Such figures form a considerable part of the present category. A single Elizabethan illustration will suffice.

> This morning, like the spirit of a youth
> That means to be of note, begins betimes.
> *Ant. and Cleo.* IV, 4, 26

One may paint a youth who shall stand for morning. The specific reference of the minor term is here however to the spirit of youthful enterprise. The figure is Expansive. A notable image of this sort in recent poetry is Meredith's "Darker grows the valley, more and more forgetting."

A single figure may be taken to represent the category as a whole before examining its forms and functions in detail. A familiar and climactic passage in *Henry Fifth* emphasizes a metaphorical line of great imaginative wealth and pregnancy of expression. The sentence is in part as follows.

> 'Tis not the balm, the sceptre and the ball,
> The sword, the mace, the crown imperial,
> The intertissued robe of gold and pearl,
> The farced title running 'fore the King,
> The throne he sits on, nor the tide of pomp
> That beats upon the high shore of this world, . . .
> *Hen. V,* IV, 1, 277

The abstract meaning is that while all our aspirations are shattered like waves against a headland, the triumphs of royalty pass against the walls of life without pride or splendor to tragic annihilation. Humanity is imagined as a sea assaulting a coast. Its waves are destined at most for a rapturous ascent into a foreign element, followed by extinction. Royalty moans hopelessly against these ramparts. The ardor of the King's idealism is here reconciled to the sadness of his vision. A more recent variation of this Greek figure concludes Meredith's sonnet sequence, *Modern Love.*

what evermore
Moves dark as yonder midnight ocean's force,
Thundering like ramping troops of warrior horse,
To throw that faint, thin line upon the shore.

Meredith has developed a branched metaphor. A troop of
horse is an image for the waves, which in turn are images
for broken aspiration. Shakespere's figure is more condensed but also more complex and more discriminating.
Implying the idea of tragedy in Meredith it discriminated
between those efforts which attain at least a transient
splendor and those which pass ingloriously to extinction.
In this line may be observed how readily Expansive metaphor carries emotion, lends itself to contemplation and
falls from the standpoint of language into a notably con-
tracted form.

Often the utmost imaginative value is compressed into a
single metaphorical word. Extreme condensation and gen-
erality of idea suggest the Sunken figure. A vivid realization of the image however denies its inclusion under that
head. These citations illustrate pregnant metaphor.

But thy eternal summer shall not fade!

Son. 18

Green paths of youth and love.

Daniel, *Delia,* 6

How green and fresh you are in this old world!

John, III, 4, 145

When if she grieve to gaze her in her glass,
When there presents her winter withered hue.

Daniel, *Delia,* 38

Winter's not gone yet if the wild geese fly that way.

Lear, II, 4, 46

(of old age)
Spring come to you at the farthest
In the very end of harvest.

Tem. IV, 1, 114

When that I was and a little tiny boy,
    With hey, ho, the wind and the rain,
A foolish thing was but a toy,
    For the rain it raineth every day.

T. N. V, 1, 397

The bird is dead
That we have made so much on.

Cym. IV, 2, 197

In these figures summer is the symbol of ripened beauty; green paths are the ways of youth and love; a young man among old men is like a branch of fresh green in the aging year; a decaying beauty is like the withered landscape in winter. Subtler still are the images from *King Lear* and *The Tempest*. The first includes under the thought of the flight of birds and winter all the misfortunes which the Fool forbodes for Lear. In Feste's song at the conclusion of *Twelfth Night* the refrain symbolizes the recurrence of misfortune. A vein of naïve philosophy underlies the entire lyric. The Fool has justly been described as shaking his bells in a sabbath air. The wealth of suggestion in the lines from *Cymbeline* can only be realized when one recalls the fitness of the metaphor on the lips of Imogen's huntsman brother uttering his cry of pain at her supposed death. Very naturally he associates the short life of a tamed bird with the brief but dear life of his new friend. A point of pathos is touched in one metaphorical word of great simplicity.

Such figures expansive to the imagination but condensed in expression may be contrasted with those which are no less expansive to the mind than in the utterance. The accumulative character of the suggestion is born out by a rhythmical afflatus, or, in the language of Nash, by "surged harmonies."

Let Rome in Tiber melt, and the wide arch
Of the rang'd empire fall!

Ant. and Cleo. I, 1, 33

In the language of emotion may be observed Expansive figures with an effect of beauty, vigor or terror.

Images of beauty when introduced into the drama with profusion at the expense of dramatic vigor may cloy. Much of the closet drama of the nineteenth century shows the questionable depletion of energy by metaphor, an enervation in style by a profusion of rich images. The metaphor of beauty in the Elizabethan drama however is almost without exception a tonic. The plays are concentrated on character. The stage itself was relatively bare. The suggestion of physical beauty then comes largely through metaphor. By this means dialogue is elevated and stimulated to an otherwise unattainable pitch of poetry. Here are some Expansive images of beauty.

> Sometimes we see a cloud that's dragonish,
> A vapour sometime like a bear or lion,
> A tower'd citadel, a pendent rock,
> A forked mountain, or blue promontory
> With trees upon't, that nod unto the world,
> And mock our eyes with air. Thou hast seen these signs.
> They are black vesper's pageants.
>   Ay, my lord.
> That which is now a horse, even with a thought
> The rack dislimns, and makes it indistinct
> As water is in water.
>   It does, my lord.
> My good knave Eros, now thy captain is
> Even such a body.
>   *Ant. and Cleo.* IV, 14, 2

>   beauty's ensign yet
> Is crimson in thy lips and in thy cheeks,
> And death's pale flag is not advanced there.
>   *Rom. and Jul.* V, 3, 94

> And in the morn and liquid dew of youth
> Contagious blastments are most imminent.
>   *Ham.* I, 3, 41

To the series of tragic scenes which follow in rapid succession Antony's elaborate image is a gorgeous introduction. Like Romeo's image of enthusiasm and the tender lines addressed to Ophelia it not only possesses great range of beauty in itself but is true to character and dramatic situation. The following are figures of the same type from other than dramatic sources.

Save that my soul's imaginary sight
Presents thy shadow to my sightless view,
Which, like a jewel hung in ghastly night,
Makes black night beauteous and her old face new.

Son. 27

(of ships at Yarmouth)
That which especiallest nourisht the most prime pleasure in me was after a storm when they were driven in swarms, and lay close pressed together as thick as they could pack; the next day following, if it were fair, they would cloud the whole sky with canvass, and make a braver show of the sun upon them than so many banners and streamers displayed against the sun on a mountain top.

Nash, III, 158

The chiaroscuro of the first citation is a match for Rembrandt. The figure from Nash's *Praise of the Red Herring of Yarmouth* illustrates the poetic afflatus of our bohemian humorist. The artificial sonnet and the realistic pamphlet are supported by an appropriate and striking imagery.

Terror and power ally themselves to beauty. Consider some of the Expansive metaphors that bind to Elizabethan poetry the wings of speed and strength.

Betwixt two charming words, comes in my father
And like the tyrannous breathing of the north
Shakes all our buds from growing.

Cym. I, 3, 35

'Twill out, 't will out! I peace!
No, I will speak as liberal as the north!

Oth. V, 2, 219

> Not the dreadful spout
> Which shipmen do the hurricano call,
> Constring'd in mass by the almighty sun,
> Shall dizzy with more clamour Neptune's ear
> In his descent, than shall my prompted sword
> Falling on Diomed.
>
> *T. C.* V, 2, 171

Faster than spring-time showers comes thought on thought,
And not a thought but thinks on dignity.

II Hen. VI, III, 1, 337

> thou mayst prove
> To shame unvulnerable, and stick i' the wars
> Like a great sea mark, standing every flaw,
> And saving those that eye thee.
>
> *Cor.* V, 3, 72

. . . that thou dids't know how many fathom deep I am in love! But it cannot be sounded. My affection hath an unknown bottom, like the bay of Portugal.

A. Y. L. I. IV, 1, 211

These figures expressive of vigorous and powerful feeling illustrate the dynamic character of the Expansive form. The tyranny of Cymbelene, the courage of Emilia, undaunted in the face of death, the sword of Troilus' revenge, the hot impetuosity of thoughts rushing through the mind of the conspirator, York, the noble prayer of Coriolanus to the god of soldiers for his infant son, and finally the enthusiastic confession bursting from the lips of Rosalind are expressions through the Expansive metaphor of abundant and multiform energy. Only a mature art such as Shakespere's could keep what is potentially a somewhat violent figure, the sword and waterspout, from metaphorical fustian. This mass constringed by the almighty sun and dizzying the sea with clamor, however, is surely a genuine conception of impassioned and poetic imagination. It may be well to glance at these figures from the standpoint of definition and to distinguish them from the Intensive figure discussed in the preceding chapter. To paint the tyrannous and liberal breathing of the north, the terrifying clamor of the waterspout, the rapid succession of warm showers, the flaws that assault a great sea mark, and the unfathomable gulf of Portugal, and to relate these objects to an angry father, a defiance of punishment, the wrath of a betrayed lover, the mental activity of an acute intriguer, the chieftain in battle or the heroine in love might give the boldest artist pause. The metaphors remain for Shakespere the poet and for the psychology of Expansive metaphor.

The image of terror is often a Direct figure. A black scene is painted for an impending crime. This is at bottom thoroughly metaphorical. The principle scenes in the anonymous play, *Arden of Feversham,* scenes in Webster, Chapman and Tourneur, and especially in *Macbeth* are illustrations of a metaphorical setting for crime. Thus in *Macbeth:*

> light thickens, and the crow
> Makes way to the rooky wood.
> Good things of day begin to droop and drowse.
> III, 2, 49

The following images of terror are less impressionistic.

> Now o'er the one half world
> Nature seems dead.
> *Mac.* II, 1, 49

> Up, up, and see
> The great doom's image! Malcolm! Banquo!
> *Mac.* II, 3, 82

> Hell is empty
> And all the devils are here!
> *Tem.* I, 2, 214

The time and my intents are savage wild,
More fierce and inexorable far
Than hungry tigers or the roaring sea.

Rom. and Jul. V, 3, 37

O Spartan dog,
More fell than anguish, hunger or the sea!

Oth. V, 2, 362

Heaven's face doth glow,
Yea, this solidity and compound mass,
With tristful visage, as against the doom,
Is thought-sick at the act!

Ham. III, 4, 48

The reading of death on the face of nature is an Expansive figure of high imaginative comprehension. Even stronger in such activity is the metaphor which makes the face of the dead Duncan an image for the great doom itself. All the terrors of the medieval hell serve as imagery in *The Tempest*. The quotation from *Romeo and Juliet* may be contrasted with that from *Othello*. The figures are alike in theme. The first inclines toward the sensational and conventional. The rigorously condensed images from *Othello* illustrate Shakespere's packed, mature style. The citation from *Hamlet* shows how metaphor aids in the expansion of the moral imagination, associating dramatic situation and moral law. The shame of a son for a mother suggests the blush of nature for mankind.—These will suffice as illustrations of the Expansive imagery appealing chiefly to the emotions.

So far as a scientific distinction between fancy and imagination is possible, the figures of the death of nature and the vision of doom from *Macbeth* and the blush of heaven from *Hamlet* are valuable to place upon the scale of imagination. With the mechanical, transient, pedantical and ingenious conceit, the surprising but exquisitely appropriate and unfatiguing image of fancy has already been contrasted. This contrast however does not distinguish fancy from the type of imagination represented in the citations from the tragedies. The subject matter of fancy can, I believe, be fairly well distinguished from that of imagination. Any distinctions in the process of thought, either from the literal or the metaphorical aspects, must remain largely beyond our reach. What the distinction in subject matter is may be judged by contrasting the three citations from the tragedies and Mercutio's images for Queen Mab. The tragic figures carry the imagination on vast excursions comprehending the whole course of time, the all evolving moment of doom, a universal conception of death and the imagined shame of nature for mankind. Fancy may carry us far to sea, but leaves a slender track rapidly vanishing on the waters. Movement may be rapid, but the horizon is restricted. The world of the wonderful inhabited by fancy and the world of wonder inhabited by imagination are mutually exclusive. Fancy is unmoral and particularized. Imagination has not without justice been called a moral quality, from which we may assume it to be a generalizing quality. The images which fancy calls forth are denied the comprehensive imaginative value belonging to the higher types of poetic metaphor. Thus Mercutio's figure for Queen Mab, the agate on an alderman's forefinger, is fanciful less because it represents a minute object well defined in space than because it represents an idea of no known consequence, but presumably, outside of the kingdom of Queen Mab, of no consequence at all. Why is she no bigger than an agate stone, or why the agate stone on the forefinger of an alderman? The idea is excellent, but if there is any known reason for its felicity it is that it has no reason. This is not our world. We know no more of it than the poet tells us for the moment, for nothing in this world of fancy proceeds reasonably from its premises. From no one incident can we

build another nor in any one metaphor of fancy comprehend a range of experience in fairy-land. The images of
fancy are enjoyed instantaneously and not improbably at
the full. The three tragic figures on the contrary permit
no end to the task of realization. Omniscience alone could
hold them at their full value. A fine fancy may be imperishable, but a sublime metaphor of the imagination like
the three cited from *Hamlet* and *Macbeth* are ultimately
unattainable. They admit only that approximate realization which rereading and experience mature.

The following images may be tested by the foregoing observations.

> When you do dance I wish you
> A wave o' the sea, that you might ever do
> Nothing but that.
>
> *W. T.* IV, 4, 140

> A lover may bestride the gossamer
> That idles in the wanton summer air,
> And yet not fall; so light is vanity.
>
> *Rom. and Jul.* II, 6, 18

> (fantasy)
> Which is as thin of substance as the air,
> And more inconstant than the wind, who wooes
> Even now the frozen bosom of the north,
> And, being anger'd, puffs away from thence,
> Turning his face to the dew dropping south.
>
> *Rom. and Jul.* I, 4, 99

> The flame o' the taper
> Bows toward her, and would underpeep her lids.
>
> *Cym.* II, 2, 19

These figures show a world that is not our world. To dance
forever as a wave, to stride the gossamer, to ride the air, or
to receive homage from a taper one must enter the realm
of enchantment. Though imperishable, such fancies are

the delicacies of a moment. They fail to stir the imagination deeply less because of the structure than because of the content of the thought.

In strong contrast with the images of fancy are the Expansive figures of reflection. Their prevalence in Elizabethan literature even among the lesser poets and the bohemian writers shows the zest of a large public for some form of a poetic philosophy. These figures are to be distinguished from the conventional embodiment of religious and secular ideals examined under the head of the Intensive image. Emblems and personifications readily give form to familiar conceptions or set up a sign under which an accepted faith advances. Obvious limitations make difficult in such a technique an elaborate development of ideas. The Expansive figure on the contrary is relatively unpolished and incapable of receiving a popular following. It works from the mine of thought a rough ore which may later be minted by a theology, and in the more finished form of the Intensive image disseminated by means of poetic or external ritual. Of some thirty figures to be cited under this head nearly half are from Shakespere. These four may be examined with particular attention.

> But thought's the slave of life, and life time's fool.
> > *I Hen. IV,* V, 4, 81

> and blest are those
> Whose blood and judgment are so well commingled
> That they are not a pipe for Fortune's finger
> To sound what stop she please.
> > *Ham.* III, 2, 73

> When I consider everything that grows
> Holds in perfection but a little moment,
> And this huge stage presenteth nought but shows
> Whereon the stars in secret influence comment . . .
> > *Son.* 15

> but we worldly men
> Have miserable, mad, mistaking eyes.
>
> *Tit. And.* V, 2, 65

All metaphor is thought progressing with great rapidity along somewhat indeterminate paths. In no case is thought more packed than in the great images of reflection. Because of the intellectual element in these figures, however, the line of thought leaves footprints more readily tracked than in the case of images more largely emotional. Nothing better illustrates the intricacy and vigor of figurative thought than a sympathetic dissection of the poetic images of reflection.

The first of these, one recalls, is among the lines of Hotspur spoken at the point of death on the field of Shrewsbury. The most boyish and impetuous of Shakespere's soldiers becomes on the field of battle an eloquent theorist. We know the line true to character. Hotspur who in battle showed a burning zeal for danger was before the conflict the most calm and deliberate of counselors. The age of the poet itself was contemplative on the one hand and boyish, impetuous and violent on the other. The poet, sympathising with all its moods, gives reflective lines to the dare-devil soldier who contends over the ninth part of a hair. The wide dissemination of the spirit of reflective poetry over Elizabethan England materially enhanced the distinction of Elizabethan metaphor. From Marlowe, with his pagan philosophy and his sublime atheism, the drama shows a rising tendency toward reflective passages, especially in the soliloquies. And these passages are as a rule highly figurative.

The preceding figures have been images for life itself. Less comprehensive in significance though as powerful in imaginative activity are such lines as these.

> Humanity must perforce prey on itself,
> Like monsters in the deep.
>
> *Lear,* IV, 2, 49

And when we in our viciousness grow hard—
O misery on't.—the wise Gods seal our eyes;
In our own filth drop our clear judgments, make us
Adore our errors, laugh at's while we strut
To our confusion.

Ant. and Cleo. III, 13, 111

Despair for the atrocities of men who violently pursue their
fellows finds noble expression in the lines from *King Lear*.
The tragedy of Antony's infatuation, the debasing of his
judgment in his viciousness by the stern justice of nature,
is here condensed into a single metaphor. Elsewhere in
the play Antony and Augustus contrast their views of life
in powerful and still more pregnant figurative expression.
"Be a child o' the time," says Antony. "Possess it, I'll
make answer," replies Augustus. Again the pith of the
tragedy is given in imagery.

Here are two reflective and Expansive images from the
material of religion.

I am for the house with the narrow gate . . . but many will
be too chill and tender, and they'll be for the flowery way that
leads to the broad gate and the great fire.

All's Well, IV, 5, 52

Fears and scruples shake us.
In the great hand of God I stand, and thence
Against the undivulg'd pretense I fight
Of treason's malice!
                    And so do I.
                            So all.
Mac. II, 3, 135

The lines from *All's Well That Ends Well* fall to the part
of Lavache, one of Shakespere's clowns who consistently
stumbles on the imagery of ideas. One recalls also that
Autolycus, the classical and unblushing knave and jester,
on his entrance in *A Winter's Tale* gives in implied metaphor the philosophy of Vagabondia.

> But shall I go mourn for that, my dear?
> The pale moon shines by night;
> And when I wander here and there
> I then do most go right.
>
> IV, 3, 15

Another figure by implication rather than by direct intent occurs in Lear's line, ''When the thunder would not peace at my bidding '' (IV, 6, 104). Lear in this tragic recollection is not thinking alone of the thunder. The impotence of man to have his will is the burden of the King's reflection. The physical universe of which thunder is the symbol is heedless of the will of man.

Two more reflective images may close our citations from Shakespere. The inconsequential character of his *Midsummer-Night's Dream* and by implication of much else in life is symbolized in the first. The second suggests that if his reflections lead to many cheerless metaphors, the sum of their effect is not to make life more bitter but to minister a balm.

> These things seem small and undistinguishable,
> As far-off mountains turned into clouds.
>
> *M. S. N. D.* IV, 1, 191

> I'll give thee armour to keep off that word;
> Adversity's sweet milk, philosophy,
> To comfort thee, though thou art banished.
>
> *Rom. and Jul.* III, 3, 54

Chapman is relatively quite as prolific in reflective imagery as Shakespere. These citations are representative of his Expansive and reflective metaphor.

> leave my soul to me, whom it concerns;
> You have no charge of it; I feel her free;
> How she doth rouse, and like a falcon stretch
> Her silver wings, as threatning death with death,
> At whom I joyfully will cast her off.
>
> *Byron's Tragedy,* V, 4, 27

My sun is turn'd to blood, in whose red beams
Pindus and Ossa, hid in drifts of snow,
Laid on my heart and liver, from their veins
Melt like two hungry torrents eating rocks
Into the ocean of all human life,
And make it bitter only with my blood.
                    Bussy D'Ambois, V, 4, 135

Give me a spirit that on life's rough sea
Loves to have his sails filled with a lusty wind,
Even till his sail-yards tremble, his mast crack,
And his rapt ship run on her side so low
That she drinks water, and her keel ploughs air.
                Byron's Conspiracy, III, 3, 135

A worthy man should imitate the weather
That sings in tempests, and being clear is silent.
                    Bussy D'Ambois, IV, 2, 118

The first two citations are not images which Johnson would
have called "just." They do however give a just impression of the spirit of daring which animates the scene.
They are essentially just without being literally so. The
enthusiasm by which a metaphor of Chapman overshoots
the mark of his idea allies his figures to the headlong im-
petuosities of Violent imagery. Mere fustian however the
images of "the High Priest of Homer" seldom become.
They are turgid and confused. Force entangles itself with
strength. But the fury is not sham.

Let us consider the second image in detail. The blood
upon the body of the wounded D'Ambois in no strict sense
resembles torrents eroding the rocks of snow-clad Pindus
and Ossa. Strictly interpreted these mountains might
seem to be the heart and liver of the dying hero. The
meaning of the last two lines is clearly that the one legacy
which D'Ambois leaves to the world is the bitter story of
his death. The lines may be briefly interpreted. Shakespere's figure of the stars which comment on the stage of

man may not be interpreted in many times its own length.
A common difficulty in reading Shakespere is to capture
the kernel of his pregnant metaphors. His figures are difficult through condensation, Chapman's through extension.
Thus of the six lines of this citation the first four are purely
impressionistic, and leave the entire figure vague and dilated. The last two citations are, of course, far less eccentric.

Webster like Chapman is lavish in the use of metaphor
in reflective passages. His figures however are as a rule
concise and rarely confused.

> My soul like to a ship in a black storm
> Is driven I know not whither.
>
> 50
>
> I am acquainted with sad misery
> As the tanned galley slave is with his oar.
> 86
>
> We think caged birds sing when indeed they cry.
> 46

Some striking Expansive images of reflection occur in the
Introduction of Sir John Davies' philosophical poem,
Nosce Teipsum. Of these the following is representative.

> We that acquaint ourselves with every zone
>   And pass both tropics and behold each pole,
> When we come back are to ourselves unknown,
>   And unacquainted still with our own soul.

A discovery in the soul is a land-fall in the South Seas!
With the philosophical verse of Sir John Davies may be
associated the meditative verse and prose of Fulke Greville,
Lord Brooke. In his *Life of Sir Philip Sidney* are found
these figures, no less typical of their author than of his age.

. . . if the excellent image-maker had lived to finish and
bring to perfection the extraordinary frame of our common-

wealth. . . . I say what a large field an active, able spirit should have had to walk in.

I

. . . to the end that in tribute I owe him our nation may see a sea mark raised upon this native coast above the level of any private Pharos abroad; and so by a right meridian line of their own learn to sail through the straits of true virtue into the calm and spacious ocean of human honor.

I

Sir Francis Bacon presents one of the most remarkable bodies of imagery attributable to any writer in the lifetime of Shakespere. In his metaphor he "set the very wings of reason to his heels." All critics of Bacon agree in emphasizing the poetic as well as the technical value of such writing as *The Advancement of Learing* or the *Filum Labyrinthi*. A part of the glory of Bacon is the success with which he discloses Science as an ideal worthy of devotion. He was her first poet in England and remains there perhaps to this day her best. But a large measure of his eloquence lies in his figurative language. His metaphors may be compared to the flying buttresses of a gothic cathedral which are a support as well as an adornment. The gift which Taylor brought later to theology and Burke to political justice, Bacon brought to science: an imagery at once ennobled by its theme and ennobling it. If it be true that the power of an image increases with the weight of its subject, the artful figures of Bacon may well be regarded as a summit in the record of the Expansive metaphors of philosophy. The following citations must suffice to represent them.

Therefore no doubt the sovereignity of man lieth hid in knowledge, wherein many things are reserved which kings with their treasure cannot buy nor with their force command; their spials and intelligencers can give no news of them, their seamen and discoverers cannot sail where they grow.

In Praise of Knowledge

As if according to the innocent play of children the Divine Majesty took delight to hide his works, to the end to have them found out; and as if kings could not obtain a greater honor than to be God's playfellows in that game.

Advancement of Learning, Part I

As if there were sought in knowledge a couch whereon to rest a searching and restless spirit, or a terrace for a wandering and variable mind to walk up and down with a fair prospect, or a tower of state for a proud mind to raise itself upon, or a fort or commanding ground for strife and contention, or a shop for profit and sale, and not a rich storehouse for the glory of the Creator and the relief of man's estate.

Ib.

So that if the invention of the ship was thought so noble, which carrieth riches and commodities from place to place and consociateth the most remote regions in fortification of their fruits, how much more are letters to be magnified, which as ships pass through the vast seas of time, and make ages so distant to participate of the wisdom, illumination and inventions, the one of the other.

Ib.

VIII

THE EXUBERANT IMAGE

The Exuberant image is characterized by the impressionistic relation of two broad and imaginatively valuable terms. These terms though in an entirely aesthetic relation parallel each other as the parts of an analogy. The Exuberant figure may be contrasted with the Expansive by supposing two broad and smooth surfaces in a face-to-face contact and two such surfaces not only in close contact but interlocking at some critical points. A typical Exuberant figure is spoken by Marlowe's Faustus at the sight of the ghost of Helen.

> Oh thou art fairer than the evening air
> Clad in the beauty of a thousand stars!
> *Doctor Faustus*, XIII, 104

Both ideas are here of high imaginative value. Beauty is opposed to beauty. There is no other element in the metaphor. To such a powerful but impressionistic image may be opposed a series of figures previously examined as representing the highest type of Expansive metaphor. In a sentence from Bacon's *Advancement of Learning* seven metaphors are used with specific as well as accumulative effect. Bacon accuses Scholasticism of assuming that the motive for study is a love of retirement, variety, pride, contention or greed, and of forgetting that the true motive is the glory of God and the relief of human ills. These conceptions are enlivened and enforced in figures pregnant in linguistic form and Expansive in imaginative effect. The philosopher directs his metaphor to the precise points at which his enemies' armour is weak. The disciplined images of Bacon contrast sharply with the Exuberant image cited from Marlowe.

In the chapter dealing with the Violent metaphor we observed the distinction between the fustian figures of melodrama and Marlowe's pure Helicon. The fustian in literature is the profane, and where beauty is profanation comes with difficulty. The spirit of the beautiful dominates Marlowe's figures. She is, indeed, the presiding deity over that doctrine of pagan exuberance under which Marlowe abandoned the teachings of medieval Christianity, espoused the spirit of the Renaissance and heralded the poetry and philosophy of the great Elizabethan stage. His poetry, to use his own language, is a throne

> Where Beauty, Mother of the Muses, sits,
> And comments volumes with her ivory pen.
>
> *I Tamb.* V, 144

Though there may be extravagance in his figures there is unquestionably a fine exuberance, which proclaims them of the Muses. Consider for example his metaphor for dawn:

> The horse that guide the golden eye of heaven
> And blow the morning from their nosterils.
>
> *II Tamb.* IV, 4, 7

The Exuberant is also to be distinguished from the Intensive figure. When the same object which contributes the minor term to an Intensive metaphor becomes dilated by enthusiasm to supernatural activity the figure becomes Exuberant. In the lines cited from *Doctor Faustus*, for instance, the midnight air casts its veil about the ghost of Helen while the spirit pervades the darkness. An essential point in the description of the Intensive image is that the emblem shall retain its integrity of outline and significance. An intellectual discipline is required in holding the emblem at arm's length from the primary idea. The two are never confused. In the psychology of the

Exuberant Dionysian image this discipline collapses, resulting in those passages which seem to have been in Drayton's mind when he wrote of the dramatist thus:

> Marlowe bathed in the Thespian springs
> Had in him those brave, translunary things
> That the first poets had.

Of this character is the celebrated line which Barabas addresses to Abagail on the balcony: "But stay, what star shines yonder in the east?" This Drayton, no doubt, would have said shows the fine madness which rightly should inhabit the poet's brain.

The present category is better understood if considered from the outset in its historical relations. It is especially prominent in much early poetry. Barabas sees a new star in heaven when his daughter looks from the window of her convent with money bags in her hands. Mythology discovers the bodies of heroes shining in the firmament. When Helen bids farewell to Hector on the walls of Troy "her handmaid went bearing in her bosom the tender boy, the little child, Hector's loved sun, like unto a beautiful star." Here are two Exuberant Epigrams from the exceedingly large number to be found in The Greek Anthology.

> Would I were a pink rose, that fastening me with thine hands
> thou mightest grant me grace of thy snowy breast.
> Anon.

> On the stars thou gazest, my Star; would I were heaven to
> look at thee with many eyes.
> Attributed to Plato

Pagan is an epithet which may be ascribed to such imagery. It may be associated with early poetry and with those later poets who like Marlowe touch earth again and catch the glow of paganism.

The form shows four notable variations. In the first

place will be cited metaphors in which beauty is opposed
to beauty, as a rule the physical to the physical world, but
at times the physical to the subjective. Then will be observed those Exuberant hyperboles, or extravagant comparisons, magnifying the number, proportion or worth of
what is prized or feared. Next will be considered those
Exuberant figures based on a confusion of the senses.
These are especially prevalent in religious poetry. Finally
will be examined the Exuberant image when complicated
by animism, as in the two Epigrams just cited from The
Greek Anthology. This order is chosen because through
it runs an ascending scale toward more and more pagan
and apparently primitive thought. Thus figures in Exuberant animism seem most difficult of the four types for
the modern imagination to compass. Under the influence
of Marlowe's fiery lines however one willingly suspends
even here any element of disbelief and follows in the train
of the poet's rapture. The first of these types is one which
a neo-classical poet cannot achieve even if he should wish it;
the three succeeding types a neo-classical poet would not
wish to achieve even if he could.

The following images oppose physical beauty to physical
beauty. They are typified, it will be recalled, in the exclamation of Faustus on first seeing the ghost of Helen.

> Zenocrate, lovelier than the love of Jove,
> Brighter than is the silver Rhodope,
> Fairer than whitest snow on Scythian Hills.
>> *I Tamb.* I, 2, 87

> As looks the sun through Nilus' flowing stream, . . .
> So looks my lordly love, fair Tamburlaine.
>> Ib. III, 2, 47

> If all the crystal gates of Jove's high court
> Were opened wide and I might enter in
> To see the state and majesty of heaven,
> It could not more delight me than your sight.
>> *II Tamb.* I, 3, 152

Madam, sooner shall fire consume us both,
Than scorch a face so beautiful as this,
In frame of which Nature has showed more skill
Than when she gave eternal chaos form,
Drawing from it the shining lamps of heaven.

Ib. III, 4, 73

And from her countenance behold you might
A kind of twilight break, which through the air,
As from an orient cloud, glimpsed here and there;
And round about the chamber this false morn
Brought forth the day before the day was born.

Hero and Leander, II, 318

Thou fair young man, whose hair shines in mine eye
Like golden wires on David's ivory lute.

Peele, II, 38

Nor doth the milk-white way in frosty night
Appear so fair and beautiful in sight
As doen these fields and groves and sweetest bowers.

Peele, II, 10

Like to Diana in her summer weed
Girt with a crimson robe of brightest dye,
        Goes fair Samela.
Whiter than be the flocks that straggling feed
Where washed by Arethusa faint they lie
        Is fair Samela.
As fair Aurora in her morning grey
Deckt with the ruddy glister of her love
        Is fair Samela.
Like lovely Thetis on a calmed day
Whenas her brightness Neptune's fancies move
        Shines fair Samela.

Greene, Menaphon

Or gorgeous clouds upon the sun's decline.

Greene, Menaphon

In her face one might discry
The curious beauty of the sky.

Greene, Never Too Late

Unto the boundless ocean of thy beauty. . . .
                              Daniel, *Delia,* 1

For thou wilt lie upon the wings of night
Whiter than new snow on a raven's back.
                              Rom. and Jul. III, 2, 18

But truly not the morning sun in heaven
Better becomes the grey cheeks of the east,
Nor that full star that ushers in the even
Doth half that glory to the sober west.
                              Son. 132

The first citation is of interest from the standpoint of definition. The comparison of Zenocrate to the love of Jove is of course no metaphor. Neither is it metaphor to think her whiter than snow. When however she is compared to the whitest snow on Scythian hills and to the silver Rhodope, a range of snow-covered mountains in Thrace, Exuberant imagery appears. To the ideas of brightness and beauty are added the most stimulating associations. The gods themselves inhabited these mountains, leaving their visits recorded in song. The gods also dwell in whatever region Zenocrate inhabits, consecrating it in verse and legend. This is metaphorical suggestion. It is Exuberant because the terms are individually valuable to the imagination and vague but moving in their association.

The remaining figures may be considered from the power of their imaginative effect. Some are of sublime proportions, filling the walls of space to the uttermost horizon. Others, though of almost equal imaginative value, are more restricted in visual appeal. Such are those of the sun reflected in the Nile, the white snow on the raven's back and the golden wires on the ivory lute of David, the last equally suggestive to ear and eye. Of vast scope are the metaphorical pictures of the false dawn, the white flocks faint from bathing in the stream of Arethusa, the grey morning under the "ruddy glister" of the sun, the splendor of the sea in calm, gorgeous clouds, "the curious beauty of the sky," the boundless ocean, the grey east deckt with the sun, and the sober west with its full star of evening. Such splendors of earth, sea and sky the Elizabethan lovers cast at the feet of their beloved! More notable still are the third and fourth figures cited from *Tamburlaine*. In the first of these the poet sets the beauty of his love above the vision of the state and majesty of heaven's court. The image is a proclamation. Marlowe exclaims: "Behold, the true rebirth has come to England! The dreams of the mystic fall below the splendor lying within our grasp!" Thus in an Exuberant metaphor the poet renounces the glory of the Christian heaven,—nor have we any real evidence that his own proud renunciation led him like his Faustus to seek for mercy at the hands of pitiless fears. Equally astonishing is the image which throws disparagement on the art which gave form to chaos by proclaiming that a greater skill fashioned the face of Zenocrate!

The foregoing figures compare physical with physical beauty. Subtler than these are images which establish a powerful but vague relation between nature and ideas. Two of the nine ensuing citations, although outside the range of Elizabethan literature, illustrate the type at its highest effectiveness, and identify it in seventeenth and eighteenth century verse.

> the sparkling light of fame,
> Whose glory's brighter than the burnished gates
> From whence Latona's lordly son doth march,
> When mounted on his coach tinseled with flames
> He triumphs in the beauty of the heavens.
> Greene, *Orlando,* 359

> For if thy body thrive not full of thoughts
> As pure and *fiery* as Phebeus' beams. . . .
> *II Tamb.* V, 3, 237.

That grievous image of ingratitude,
That fiery thirster after sovereignty.
I Tamb. II, 6, 30

And in his eyes the fury of his heart
That shines as comets menacing revenge,
And casts a pale complexion on his cheeks,
As when the seaman sees the Hyades
Gather an army of Cimerian clouds
(Auster and Aquilon with winged steeds,
All sweating tilt about the watery heavens
With shivering spears enforcing thunderclaps,
And from their shields strike flames of lightening)
All-fearful, folds his sails, and sounds the main,
Lifting his prayers to heaven for his aid
Against the terror of the winds and waves.
I Tamb. III, 2, 73

A stately builded ship, well rigged and tall,
The ocean maketh more majestical;
Why vowest thou then to live in Sestos here,
Who on love's seas more glorious wouldst appear?
Hero and Leander

How fair she is that makes my music mount,
And every string of my heart's harp to move.
Greene, *Menaphon*

But things to come exceed our human reach,
And are not painted yet in angels' eyes.
Peele, 83

Meanwhile the mind from pleasure less,
Withdraws into its happiness; . . .
Annihilating all that's made
To a green thought in a green shade.
Marvell, *Thoughts in a Garden*

Glorious the sun in mid career;
Glorious the assembled fires appear,
    Glorious the comet's train;
Glorious the trumpet and alarm,
Glorious The Almighty's Stretched-Out Arm,
    Glorious the enraptured main:

Glorious the northern lights astream,
Glorious The Song When God's The Theme,
    Glorious the thunder's roar;
Glorious The Hosannah From The Den,
Glorious The Catholic Amen,
    Glorious The Martyr's Gore.
                    Christopher Smart, *Song of David*

The abstract ideas symbolized in these figures are succes-
sively fame, energetic thought, the zest for sovereignty,
terror suggested by the blanched cheek of a hero, beauty
majestical on the seas of passion, delight, hoped for deeds
in dim futurity, the Almighty's power, the glory of the
praise of God, the glorious Hosannah of the imprisoned
Christian, the glory of the Catholic Amen and the glory
of the martyr's gore.   These ideas are enforced by objects
of beauty powerfully but indefinitely related to them in
metaphor.   Such are sunrise, fire, an approaching storm,
a ship on the open sea, the music of a harp, the light of
recognition in the eyes of angels, the green of a garden,
sun, stars, comets, trumpets, enraptured seas, northern
lights and the roar of thunder!   Robust should be the
reader's capacity for beauty if he is to partake of imagery
from the springs of Marlowe and Smart!   Of the nine figures Peele's is perhaps the subtlest, and the Platonic image
from Marvell one of the most significant.   Symbolism of
color is essentially vague and frequently, as in Marvell's
lines, becomes Exuberant.   Yet as seen in the robes of
Fidelia, Speranza and Charissa in Spenser it contributes
to Intensive imagery in the familiar fashion of the color
allegory of the Renaissance.   In Spenser it is an assumption, an admired convention in religious devotion.   The
lines of Marvell are an experience in an exceptional meta-
physics.

The following illustrations represent the metaphorical
hyperbole of number in Marlowe.

> As many circumcised Turks we have,
> And warlike bands of Christians renied,
> As hath the ocean or the Terrene sea
> Small drops of water when the sun begins
> To join in one his semi-circled horns.
>
> *I Tamb.* **III**, 1, 8

> Nay, could their number countervail the stars,
> Or ever-drizzling drops of April showers,
> Or withered leaves that Autumn shaketh down,
> Yet would the Soldan by his conquering power
> So scatter and consume them in his rage
> That not a man should live to rue their fall.
>
> *I Tamb.* **IV**, 1, 30

These images are hyperboles, but metaphorical as well. The first describes the army of Bajazeth marshaled against Constantinople. The sea in flood has much more than a merely numerical relation to the hordes of the emperor. Stars, drops in drizzling April showers and the withered leaves of Autumn are not mere numerical counters to balance the forces of the grim Tamburlaine.

A single image will sufficiently illustrate the Exuberant hyperbole of proportion. The metaphorical element is here at its lowest possible degree, though the imagination is eminently vigorous, suggesting Milton.

> But now, Orcanes, view my royal host
> That hides the plains and seems as vast and wide
> As doth the desert of Arabia
> To those that stand on Bageth's lofty tower,
> Or as the ocean to the traveller
> That rests upon the snowy Appenines
>
> *II Tamb.* **I**, 1, 160

Here are two illustrations of the Exuberant hyperbole of worth. They are in the spontaneous language of transcendent emotion.

Were all the lofty mounts of *Zona mundi*
That fill the midst of farthest Tartary
Turned into gold and proffered for my stay
I would not bide the fury of my father.

II Tamb. III, 1, 41

If heaven would make me such another world
Of one entire and perfect chrysolite,
I'd not have sold her for it.

Oth. V, 2, 144

One of these citations falls quite unexpectedly from the lips of Tamburlaine's craven son. The other is spoken by Othello at the moment of tragic catastrophe. We recognize the power and beauty of the image from Marlowe, but also the dramatic fitness of the image from Shakespere. Especially in the Tamburlaine plays Marlowe sows his figures profusely without consideration for their dramatic appropriateness. Metaphors do not inevitably belong to a particular character or situation. The same manner may be seen in the plays of Peele and Greene written in imitation of Marlowe. Shakespere, the human, everywhere humanizes his poetry, gives each character a particular idiom and each scene and play its peculiar treatment. He transforms the early Elizabethan drama, epic in scheme and lyric in execution, into pure dramatic art. The impersonal and essentially lyric imagery in the nineteenth century closet drama follows in no respect the metaphorical manner of Shakespere, but inadvertently follows the manner of Marlowe where least adapted to dramatic form.

A type of metaphor more impressionistic than the Exuberant metaphor of beauty, color symbolism or the figurative hyperbole results from a confusion of the senses. Only in moments of rare enthusiasm do stars burst into song and sound into color. Here are two images in which stars that glitter to the eye seem musical to the ear.

There's not the smallest orb which thou behold'st
But in his motion like an angel sings,
Still quiring to the young ey'd cherubins.

M. of V. V, 1, 60

And thy sweet voice give back unto the spheres.

Daniel, *Delia,* 18

Beyond a somewhat limited number of familiar conventions the Elizabethans, with all their audacity, were not fond of such thought. Poets in the latter half of the last century and in still more recent years have viewed it with much greater favor.

An Exuberant figure often takes the form of animism. In discussing the Decorative image the pathetic fallacy was observed ingeniously used in avowedly light verse with depreciative effect. The same form appears with far different effect in the fiery lines of high-pitched poetry. One recognizes shining grains of barbaric paganism and early superstition which have in some way passed the sober filters of civilization. The bright dust of ideas that in their substance have long been crushed is still blowing in our eyes. If animism affords the most pagan forms of imagery, like the hyperbole it is frequently not metaphorical. In animism two types of thought are conspicuous. A body which is ordinarily considered inanimate may be animated, or an abstract idea transformed to a living body, which is thought of as a reality and not as the mere symbol for the idea. Thus if I say that the stars gaze on man I am animating the stars; while if I speak of the soul as a physical body temporarily lodged in a human body, a corporeal reality is given to an abstract idea. What is the relation of metaphor to these types of animism?

In the following lines inanimate bodies are conceived to live with the minds of men.

Sweet picture of divine Zenocrate
That, hanging here, will draw the gods from heaven,
And cause the stars fixed in the southern arc
(Whose lovely faces never any viewed
That have not passed the center's latitude)
As pilgrims travel to our hemisphere,
Only to gaze upon Zenocrate.

II Tamb. III, 2, 27

And with our sun-bright armour as we march
We'll chase the stars from heaven, and dim their eyes
That stand and muse at our admired arms.

I Tamb. II, 3, 22

The piteous stars may see our miseries
And drop their golden tears upon the ground.

Peele, II, 50

The comparison of the southern stars moving in unison across the expanse of the heavens to pilgrims come in silent wonder to view the picture of Zenocrate as clearly fulfills the definition of metaphor as the requirements of exalted poetry! The idea of stars that muse on the grandeur of human deeds is but another version of Plato's Epigram of Night gazing on love with a thousand eyes. Peele conceives the star-beams as tears which the heavens drop in sympathy for the miseries of men. Peele's philosophy may have met with mortality, but not his art.

The tendency to fuse matter and thought has already been observed in Marvell's beautiful, elusive and metaphorical lines that imagine the mind of the garden-lover:

Annihilating all that's made
To a green thought in a green shade.

This however is still color symbolism. Color is not animated, but thought expressed in color. A figure of Chapman's similarly lingers on the border of direct animism. Time, as with Marvell, becomes matter, and further passes

into a definite conception of space.   In *The Tears of Peace*
the poet writes, "I saw eternity's straight milk-white
way." Any possibility of personification in Chapman's
line is lacking in the well known vision of Vaughan.

> I saw eternity the other night
> Like a great ring of pure and endless light,
>   All calm as it was bright.

In Donne's *Second Anniversary* occurs a line apparently
identifying thought with matter.   The lady who has died
was so delicately beautiful, "That one might almost say
her body thought." A striking instance of the same idea
may be taken from the last words of Tamburlaine.   He is
warning his sons of the fate of Phaëton in his father's
chariot.

> Be warned by him then; learn with awful eye
> To sway a throne as dangerous as his;
> For if thy body thrive not full of thoughts
> As pure and fiery as Phyteus' beams,
> The nature of these proud rebelling jades
> Will take occasion by the slenderest hair
> And draw thee piecemeal, like Hippolytus.
>
> <div align="right">II <i>Tamb.</i> V, 3, 235</div>

This comes nearest to full animism, if not in fact attaining
it.   Here it is quite possible to see an identity of matter
and thought.   The spirit of Blake might leap at such a
metaphor.   The following additional citations are vaguely
metaphorical but purely animistic.

> Eternity was in our lips and eyes.
>
> *Ant. and Cleo.* I, 3, 35

>   say, and speak thick,—
> Love's counselor must fill the bores of hearing
> To the smothering of the senses.
>
> *Cym.* III, 2, 58

Sweet Helen, make me immortal with a kiss!
Her lips suck forth my soul; see where it flies!—
Come, Helen, come, give me my soul again!
Here will I dwell, for heaven is in these lips
And all is dross that is not Helena.

Doctor Faustus, scene 13

Comb down his hair! look! look! it stands upright,
Like lime twigs set to catch my winged soul.

II Hen. VI, III, 3, 15

Lo, now I breath upon thee! A hundred deaths come
upon thee!

Nash, I, 289

Such figures as these represent the highest reaches of impressionistic and pagan imagery. The appearance of eternity, love's thoughts, the soul and the curse remain obscure. The modern mind dimly imagines what in a primitive culture might have lived with the reality of rocks or trees. Metaphorical exuberance can go no further.

No general estimate of Exuberant imagery can be made without a contrast with other forms. While Intensive and, still more, Expansive imagery are intricate in their qualifications of ideas, the Exuberant figure paints in bold strokes. The reflection of a tree in water displays the branches at a new angle and shows the smoothness and clarity of the stream. Similarly an Intensive or Expansive metaphor is a happy coincidence of terms which profit by mutual interpretation. An Exuberant image may be illustrated by a figure which Marlowe loved, the reflection of the sun in water. Light answers light and splendor replies to splendor. The image of the sun is blurred in the water, which is itself confused in the sunlight. The effulgent metaphors of Marlowe coin new impressions for a familiar magnificence. They neither interpret themselves from within nor vary widely from one another. Beauty and power, power and beauty flash back their metaphors

from line to line. The heliostat which Shakespere turned
toward the sun of the ideal brings innumerable messages
without repetition. Marlowe held one mirror that flashed
one unalterable reply. Exuberant metaphor was a lens for
that mirror. It served the purpose of Marlowe thoroughly.
It would have been far less useful to the restless mind of
so catholic a genius as Shakespere.

Two personifications may be reconsidered in contrasting
Shakespere's manner with that of Marlowe. They are the
celebrated images of dawn.

> Night's candles are burnt out, and jocund day
> Stands tip-toe on the misty mountain tops.

> But, look, the morn, in russet mantle clad,
> Walks o'er the dew of yon high eastern hill.

The first of these citations is spoken by Romeo at his last
parting from Juliet. It is the very phrase of youthful
love. Romeo only, we fancy, could speak in precisely this
metaphor. Now contrast with this figure that spoken by
Horatio. The scene must be vividly realized to perceive
the fitness of Horatio's lines. Francisco says that the night
is bitter cold. An armed and pious guardsman, who believes that the first note of the byre-cock has caused an un-
holy ghost to vanish into the gray of morning, is conversing
with a somewhat stern and sober-minded scholar. The
watch is breaking up. The stage is prepared for a solemn
tragedy. And then the image: the morn clad in a russet
mantle walks on the dewy hill. How exquisitely appropriate are these lines both to Horatio and to the rising of
the curtain upon the tragedy of Denmark! Nowhere else
would the image be so fitting. Nowhere is the particularization of beauty more marked than in Shakespere. Exuberant imagery will not be so restrained. It hews roughly
out of the living rock. Shakespere's figures are delicately
chiseled out of the purest marble.

Finally with the Exuberant metaphors of Marlowe may be contrasted Shakespere's Expansive images of reflection, numerous illustrations of which were cited in the preceding chapter. In this chapter few images from reflective poetry would be quotable. Only in the broadest sense can any of the figures which have been cited be held to have a philosophical value. Those who place a light estimate upon reflective poetry will perhaps admire the Exuberant metaphor above all other types of imagery. Those who cherish more and hold more profound than even the rapturous verse of Marlowe the poetry represented in such a phrase as Shakespere's "ripeness is all" will regard Exuberant imagery inferior from the standpoint of poetic value, as it unquestionably is inferior in the modification of its parts by metaphorical thought. Marlowe's deep influence upon Elizabethan thought was due to the totality of his work. The plays of Shakespere have in their catholic sympathy not only a profound unity, but upon innumerable points and through innumerable metaphors contribute to our knowledge of men's variorum of life, the variorum supremely worth our reading.

IX

IMAGES OF WIT AND HUMOR

For the figure of wit and humor I shall attempt no such definition as for the types previously discussed. Habits in serious imagery are much more plastic than those in the imagery of wit and humor; and the use of serious imagery invites more conscious art. An inevitable suspicion therefore lies with some justice at the door of a detailed and highly organized discussion of the theme of this chapter. If *The Anatomy of Melancholy* has abundant wit, a protracted anatomy of wit might well become a melancholy and a dismal science.

Five types of imagery are conspicuous under this head. These are the metaphors of wit, of irony, of gothic humor, of plain incongruity and of fancy. Of these types the first two are rare in Elizabethan literature and the remaining three abundantly represented. The figure of wit delights by hitting the heart of the target. The figure of irony surprises by contradiction, by over-statement, by under-statement or even by an unlooked-for convention. The figure of gothic humor by coarse, good natured, powerful caricature appeals strongly to the eye. The figure of incongruity is a surprising comparison with one grain of similitude for ten of dissimilarity. The figure of fancy in humor is too sympathetic to be a Decorative conceit, not sympathetic enough to be an Expansive figure, delicate and airy enough to be fancy and audacious and surprising enough to be humor. Metaphors of wit and incongruity are related to the Radical image. The figure of gothic humor is often highly Expansive in imaginative value. These types may be viewed more precisely as varieties of

206

the preceding categories than as one or more categories themselves. An opportunity is thus afforded to glance backward over the completed discussion of the serious figures and to test to some degree the meaning of previous distinctions.

Many a humorous image is of marked poetic value. It may possess rare beauty. A jocular proverbial saying recorded in *The Merry Wives of Windsor* is clearly regarded as a humorous fancy and as clearly possessed of unusual loveliness. "A man may hear this shower singing in the wind." The farmers of Stratford joking about the weather afforded poetry which Shakespere could do no better than to accept. The popular metaphor of the English countryside compares more than favorably from the standpoint of imaginative value with the courtly images of Lyly. The domestic humor approaches the Expansive form, and belongs to the native Middle English tradition. The courtly humor approaches the Decorative category and belongs to Renaissance fashions abroad. These represent the two principal veins of light metaphor in the period. The preference of the modern reader is almost inevitably for the more democratic. English genius for the spoken metaphor doubtless needed refinement in the time of Queen Bess; but English had a richer stock for development at home than any of the fantastic shoots of aristocratic wit grafted from abroad. Evidences of homely humor that set lightly on strong stomachs are too abundant in sixteenth century prose to require extended illustration. Writers of prose for the people sow gratuitously at every stride images of an eminently strong savor. Thus Nash speaking of a student over-prepared for college calls him " rotten-ripe." Criticizing the conceited courtier and traveller who praises Spain and defames his native land, Nash says that he "makes a dishcloth of England." The champion of the red herring would have unmercifully lashed such impotent

words as "over-prepared" or "disloyal." A coarse imagery was required properly to fortify and invigorate a
popular prose style.

Before discussing the types of imagery in wit and humor
a preliminary sketch of the figurative manner of Thomas
Nash, who has been chosen to play the leading rôle in this
chapter, may be suggestive. Nash resolutely turned his
back on the patches of Euphuistic figures, which like patches
of sweet peas in a garden harmlessly decorate the pages of
Lyly. The greatest Elizabethan prose humorist, arming
himself with a most formidable vocabulary of continental
derivatives, entrenched himself behind the native humor of
the English people. He hated a foolish Euphuisum and
pedantic imitations of the pedantic Guevara as bitterly as
he hated the courtier who praised Spain and debased England. Gabriel Harvey in a luckless moment accused him
of plagiarising Euphuistic metaphors. Nash cracks his
whip:

Is my style like Greene's or my jests like Tarlton's? Do I
talk of any counterfeit birds or herbs or stones or rake up new
found poetry from under the walls of Troy? . . . Euphues I
read when I was a little ape in Cambridge, and then I thought
it *ipse ille*. It may be excellent good still for ought I know,
but for I lookt not in it this ten year. But to imitate it I
abhor.

I, 319

The spirit of Nash's metaphor is not far to seek. Everywhere a spontaneous exercise of the imagination for the joy
of it characterizes this bohemian scholar and prose poet.
This is his ironical critique on his own style.

For I mean to come upon him with a tempest of thunder and
lightning worse than the storms in the West Indies called the
Furicanoes. . . . Gentlemen, what think you of this sober,
mortified style?

III, 20

Here is the keynote of Elizabethan humor. Nash's metaphors in his most boisterously humorous passages are often
the purest gold of poetry. In him we see the realist and
the humorist which time or temperament left undeveloped
in Marlowe. The humor of poetic exuberance typifies both
Nash and his age.

A polished imagery of wit, the foil of intellectual comedy,
is, accordingly, rare in Elizabethan literature. Here is
found the comedy of mirth and fun. If there is satire, it
is broad, not precise or discriminating. Fancy and all that
expands the imagination and sends the mind gambling
from sharp distinctions are its characteristics. There are
smiles, gentleness, pathos, exquisite song, hoarse laughter,
merriment and fantastic fooling. Critical comedy resembling that of Molière is at the opposite pole from these
scenes of the mirth of taverns and green fields. As our
modern Shavian comedy sells songs for epigrams, it for-
feits the metaphor of gothic humor for the keen image of
critical wit. One must not look in this comedy of excellent fooling for the pleasures which the sharper satirical
weapon affords. The Elizabethans were inclined to take
their critical thought seriously and their amusement in
rollicking. The imagery of rollicking they have developed
supremely well, the image of satire very imperfectly.
When Chapman writes of a man "quagmired in philosophy," or when Hal tells Poins that "never a man's thought
in the world keeps the roadway better than thine," we have
images as near to critical wit as the Elizabethans are accustomed to come. Even in these the poetic element is considerable. The man quagmired in philosophy admits a
romantic caricature. Hal's figure for Poins is also well on
the way to Expansive imagery. The idea of a prosaic
traveller who never steps out of the road to pluck a flower
nor ever attempts a short cut to his destination sets the
mind at the edge of an illimitable range of suggestion.

This is not the trained and rapierlike metaphor of the Frenchman. Illustrations of the figure of wit can better be taken from other than Elizabethan sources. Swift stands midway between a fanciful and an intellectual humor, with the strength of each. When however he writes, "eloquence smooth and cutting is like a razor whetted with oil," we have the essence of the image of wit. Yet the finest humor is greater because more synthetic than the finest wit. Millamant's epigrams are wit only, Falstaff's images are body, wit and soul.

To the metaphor of wit that of irony is intimately related. Precision characterizes each. Indeed the image of irony, though requiring more essential imagination than the common figure of wit, may be even more delicately adjusted. It is achieved by over-statement, by under-statement, by ironical convention and by a violent but artful contrast of ideas. Exaggeration is abundant in Elizabethan images of humor, but much more often frankly exuberant than delicate and ironical. An instance of ironical under-statement, that trope dear to the English mind from Beowulf to Hosea Biglow, occurs in the talk of Shakespere's Antony at the banquet on the ship of Pompey. Though it is not an Egyptian feast, Antony assures his host that it "ripens toward it." An instance of wit arising from mock conventionality appears in the same scene. Antony ironically warns the failing "third part of the world," "These quicksands, Lepidus!" More familiar are figures based on violent but artful contrasts. Nash for example speaks of the jail as a "castle of contemplation." Of a similar sort is a phrase in Mr. G. M. Trevelyan's book, *The Poetry and Philosophy of George Meredith*. Meredith, he says, wages against the ego a metaphorical war to the knife, thus hinting that we are not to take the poet's pronouncements in too strict a sense. Of a similar sort would be such an observation as the following. "The five

exceptions in the development of this diphthong from Old
English may be called melodramatic.'' One does not commonly associate melodrama and linguistic studies. These
more delicate forms of irony are infrequent in the literature of the Elizabethans. When images of wit and irony
appear in that literature, they have as a rule a strong
coloring of gothic humor.

This prevailing type of humor and imagery may be
traced from the prose of the later Middle Ages. Such a
little book as Gerard Leeu's version of the Dialogue of
Solomon and Marcolphus well represents it. The metaphor
of gothic humor may be observed under three heads.
There are figures which without the edge of the image of
irony or its discipline or restraint suggest it in incongruity
and depreciative intent. Second, there is that great body
of images where imagination passes from the physical to
the physical world, frequently heaping deformity on deformity and drawing a great, generous and simple hearted
laugh. Finally there are those metaphors of humor which
in spite of a strong appeal to the grotesque imagination
carry a genuine weight of criticism. Let not the intellectual scorn these metaphors. They are the metaphors of
Rabelais.

A few figures of each type may be examined. These
present ideas in grotesque antithesis.

> Dids't thou never see Titan kiss a dish of butter?
> *I Hen. IV*, II, 4, 133

The sun was so in his mumps upon it that it was almost noon
before he could go to cart that day.

> Nash, III, 198

In these figures thought is confined to the physical world.

(of Justice Shallow)
I do remember him at Clement's Inn like a man made after
supper of a cheese paring. When 'a was naked, he was, for all

the world, like a forked radish, with a head fantastically carv'd
upon it with a knife.

II Hen. IV, III, 2, 332

Oenigmatical. . . . A word it is that the Doctor lay a whole
week and a day and a night entranced in his bed to bring
forth, and on the Monday evening late caused all the bells in
the parish . . . to be rung forth for joy that he was delivered
of it.

Nash, III, 15

O, 'tis an unconscionable vast gorbellied volume, bigger
bulkt than a pair of Swisser omnipotent galeaze breeches.
Such a huge dry-fat of duncery it is he hath dunged up against
me as was never seen since the reign of Averrois.

Ib. III, 35

This impotent answer drops from thee even as sweat from a
lean man that drinks sack.

Ib. III, 16

(men) that look as just as Jehovah by day, enthronizing grave
zeal and religion on the elevated whites of their eyes.

Ib. I, 385

a beard as though it had been made of a bird's nest pluckt in
pieces, which consisteth of straw, hair and dirt mixt together.

Ib. II, 247

After a rain conies use to come out of their holes and to sit
nibling on weeds or anything in the cool of the evening, and
after a reveling when younger brothers have spent all or in
their gaming have lost all, they sit plotting in their chambers
with necessity how to be furnished presently with a new supply
of money.

Dekker, *Lanthorne and Candlelight*, III, 231

Except it were a dog in a doublet you shall not see anyone
so disguised as are my countrymen of England.

Harrison's England, 168

If he be weasel-beakt then much hair left on the cheeks will make the owner look big like a bowled hen, and so grim as a goose.

Ib. 169

It is incredible to say how our maltbags lug at their liquor even as pigs should lie in a row lugging at their dame's teats, till they lie still again and be not able to wag.

Ib. 295

So that to meet a priest in those days was to behold a peacock that spreadeth his tail when he danceth before the hen; which now, I say, is well reformed.

Ib. 33

Do thou amend thy face, and I'll amend my life! Thou art our admiral; thou bearest the lantern in the poop, but 'tis in the nose of thee. Thou art the Knight of the Burning Lamp.

Why, Sir John, my face does you no harm.

No, I'll be sworn; I make as good use of it as many a man doth of a Death's head or a *memento mori;* I never see thy face but I think upon hell-fire and Dives that lived in purple; for there he is in his robes, burning. . . . When thou ran'st up Gadshill in the night to catch my horse, if I did not think thou had'st been an *ignis fatuus* or a ball of wildfire, there's no purchase in money. O, thou art a perpetual triumph, an everlasting bonfire light.

I Hen. IV, III, 3, 28

Then did the sun on dunghill shine!

M. W. W. I, 3, 70

What tempest, I trow, threw this whale, with so many tuns of oil in his belly, ashore at Windsor?

Ib. II, 1, 65

And in the height of this bath, when I was more stew'd in grease, like a Dutch dish, to be thrown into the Thames, and cool'd, glowing hot, in that surge, like a horse-shoe.

Ib. III, 5, 120

Do you not remember, 'a saw a flea stick on Bardolph's nose, and a' said it was a black soul burning in hell-fire?

Hen. V, II, 3, 42

. . . it is like a coal of fire, sometimes plue and sometimes red, but his nose is executed and his fire's out.

Ib. III, 6, 110

These figures show the grotesque image used with a thoroughly subjective significance and a satirical effect:

> *2 Cit.* Think you so? Which way do you judge my wit would fly?
>
> *3 Cit.* Nay, your wit will not so soon out as another man's will, 'tis so strongly wedg'd up in a block head; but if it were at liberty, 't would, sure, southward.
>
> *2 Cit.* Why that way?
>
> *3 Cit.* To lose itself in a fog, where being three parts melted away with rotten dews, the fourth would return for conscience' sake, to help to get thee a wife.

Cor. II, 3, 27

They'll take suggestion as a cat laps milk.

Tem. II, 1, 288

Those that calculated his nativity said that Saturn and the Moon . . . were melancholy conjoined together.

Nash, III, 63

This grotesque vein appears notably in the proverbial sayings of Haywood and Sir Thomas More. Appended to T. E. Bridgett's book on More for example are ninety-five of the philosopher's aphorisms. Three-fourths of these are strongly metaphorical. By far the greater number belong to the type of gothic humor. One may trace the form in such a phrase as Swift's on curiosity, "that ring in the nose of a lazy, impatient and grunting reader," or in the mock heroic games of the Second Book of *The Dunciad,* or, for example, in Poe's description of a transcendentalist as

"an old sheep in a reverie." Gothic imagery, grotesque
and bizarre as it is, is, then, by no means confined to a
merely sensuous humor.

Perhaps few authors to-day unbend to such mirth as that
of Harrison and the Lord of the Taverns. A change appears in the externals of imagery which makes the old
humor at times difficult for us. There are fewer butter
plates exposed to the sun, fewer muffle-footed carters rising
half drunk to go to work at noon; we carve fewer grotesques out of radishes and cheese parings; Poins no longer
feels poetic afflatus at the sight of dungheaps; men sweat
less often over their sherry; barbers, who flocked into England at the close of the sixteenth century and established
a more sanitary order, keep beards from a resemblance to
that unsightly object described by Harrison; city dwellers
see less of animals, "bowled hens" and "grim geese"; nor
do men so frequently lie about inns like a litter of pigs,
"not able to wag." The surface of life has been exten-
sively smoothed and altered since the uncouth days of
Elizabeth's England. Something of the spirit but much
more of the form of the old imagery has disappeared. For
amusement analogous to that which the figures just cited
afford the motion pictures are exceptionally favorable.
They too may at times give exuberant delight and generous
purgations of laughter, of much benefit to our physical if
not to our intellectual nature. Their humor also is frequently the rollicking physical fun that appears in gothic
metaphor. Although they may lack that inspiration of
sherry and covert aid of the Muses which give immortality
to Sir John, the joy of robust caricature is also theirs.

In the anthology of gothic metaphor which Falstaff be-
stows on Bardolph the relation of that form to Expansive
imagery is obvious. Another type of the figure of humor
suggests the Radical image. Although here terms are frequently more sympathetic than in the Radical image, they

still show the incongruity, ingenuity and surprise of that form. They well represent what Samuel Rowlands called "a letting of humor's blood in the headvein."

Look, he's winding up the watch of his wit; by and by it will strike.

Tem. II, 1, 12

there may be more resounding bell-metal in my pen than I am aware of.

Nash, III, 156

Home went his Beatitude's caterer with a flea in his ear.

Ib. III, 206

Two blockheads, two blunderkins, having their brains steeped in nought but balderdash . . . the dead palsy and apoplexy of the press, the sarpego and siatica of the seven liberal sciences, the surfeiting vomit of Lady Vanity, the sworn bands to one another's vain glory.

Ib. III, 11

I would not have you think that all this that is set down is in good earnest . . . for then you go the wrong way to Westminster. . . . Tell me, what do you think of this case? Am I subject to the sin of wrath . . . in whetting my pen against this block?

Ib. I, 199

A fanciful figure more sympathetic than the Decorative and less sympathetic than the Expansive form may often be regarded as an image of humor. As an illustration of this last and loveliest type of Elizabethan mirth one may quote from its master, Greene.

Some take no pleasure but in amorous passions, no delight but in madrigals of love, whetting Cupid's wings with rose water and tricking up his quiver with sweet perfumes.

VIII, 35

Five types of metaphor have now been distinguished.

The incisive, critical metaphor of wit and the figurative and pointed shafts of irony are relatively rare in Elizabethan authors. On the contrary the image of gothic humor, sensuous, grotesque, pregnant and unlicked, is the staple of Elizabethan comedy. Under an uncouth exterior, however, these Rabelaisian conceptions may have a considerable degree of satirical power. Radical antitheses are lavishly scattered among the images of humor. Finally fanciful figures of much delicacy cross and recross the homely pages like fairies playing on a homely hearth. The sixteenth century metaphor of humor is not the keen weapon of satirical fence and thrust, nor the finely adjusted figure of wit and irony, but on low note and high, from the great masculine laughter of carters and drawers to the laughter of spirits like rain "singing in the wind," the laughter of England arises from innocent mirth. Nash with his resonant laughter, Jonson with his deep-chested laughter, John Day with a silvery mirth, Greene and Dekker with their sweet, kindly, cleansing, musical tones, are all fitting accompaniments to the gentle or the mighty laughter of Shakespere. Since the greatness of the Elizabethan comedy does not lie in satire, the imagery of this comedy does not excel in the metaphor of satire. Ben Jonson gives more delight in his robust mirth, in that she-Falstaff, the pig-woman Ursula, than in his laborious and didactic scenes. The Elizabethan age excels in humor, but it is the humor of mirth, profane or delicate, of Eastcheap or of Arden, maturing to spiritual flower in Milton's *L'Allegro*.

X

SHAKESPERE

The subject of poetic imagery affords little opportunity for tabular or mechanical treatment. Compilations are easily made but are not easily made illuminating. An apology for the succeeding tables is accordingly my first comment. They show with only a fair degree of accuracy the number of well defined images in the individual plays of Shakespere, in the plays grouped as comedy, history, tragedy and romance, and in the plays arranged chronologically. No two readers of a play will find the same number of figures. Literal phrases shade almost imperceptibly into figurative. Many of the subtler images must inevitably escape notice. The grouping of the plays is also frankly superficial. The chronological order, too, is uncertain. No assurances valuable or otherwise can be based on the trebly insecure premises on which these tables rest. They are necessarily inaccurate and impressionistic studies under the deceiving guise of mathematics. In all the tables but one, therefore, I have felt free to add a still further generalizing distinction, that between figures of a superficial and a profound imaginative value. To one list belong conventional images that give the scene dignity, as decorative letters dignify an old page. To the other belong figures with a substantial stimulus to the imagination. From such a process conclusions can only be drawn in a broad way. The steady development of Shakespere's art of metaphor, an increasing number of images, his growing independence, the flexibility and unbinding of a conventionally ornate dialogue, are the chief indications of this arrangement.

218

TABLE I

Showing the Number of Figures Recorded in Each Play

Troilus and Cressida	234	As You Like It	82
Hamlet	206	I Henry VI	73
Antony and Cleopatra	200	Measure for Measure	65
Macbeth	172	The Merchant of Venice	65
Coriolanus	147	All's Well That Ends Well	64
King John	135	Twelfth Night	61
I Henry IV	133	Timon of Athens	60
II Henry VI	133	Julius Caesar	58
III Henry VI	130	A Midsummer-Night's Dream	56
Richard II	128	Titus Andronicus	56
Othello	127	Pericles	54
Richard III	127	Much Ado About Nothing	51
King Lear	125	The Merry Wives of Windsor	50
Romeo and Juliet	117	Love's Labor's Lost	46
The Winter's Tale	112	The Two Gentlemen of Verona	31
Cymbeline	103	The Taming of the Shrew	27
The Tempest	96	The Comedy of Errors	14
Henry V	96		

TABLE II

Chronological

The plays chronologically	Average number of figures recorded	Average number of highly imaginative figures	Ratio of the highly imaginative figures to total number recorded
First 9 plays	80.9	17.9	22.2%
Second 9 plays	89.2	29.9	32.0%
Third 9 plays	93.2	40.0	42.9%
Fourth 9 plays	130.9	62.2	48.8%

TABLE III

The Dramatic Types

	Average number of figures recorded	Average number of highly imaginative figures	Ratio of the highly imaginative figures to total number recorded
11 Comedies	49.5	19.5	39.3%
9 Histories	118.7	29.1	24.5%
10 Tragedies and 2 Tragi-Comedies	130.5	56.1	42.9%
4 Dramatic Romances	91.2	50.5	55.6%

TABLE IV

RATIO OF THE HIGHLY IMAGINATIVE FIGURES TO THE TOTAL NUMBER RECORDED IN EACH PLAY

The Winter's Tale	67%	Measure for Measure	33%
The Tempest	66	II Henry VI	32
The Merry Wives of Windsor	58	King John	28
Twelfth Night	57	Timon of Athens	28
Antony and Cleopatra	56	Henry V	27
Othello	55	Pericles	25
As You Like It	53	Richard II	24
The Merchant of Venice	50	All's Well That Ends Well	24
Troilus and Cressida	48	Love's Labor's Lost	24
Cymbeline	47	Titus Andronicus	23
Macbeth	47	Coriolanus	22
King Lear	45	Much Ado About Nothing	21
Hamlet	45	Julius Caesar	20
A Midsummer-Night's Dream	44	Richard III	19
Romeo and Juliet	40	The Two Gentlemen of Verona	12
I Henry IV	39	The Taming of the Shrew	11
II Henry IV	36	I Henry VI	08
		III Henry VI	07

The first table requires little comment. *Richard Second* is in one respect among the most figurative of the plays. It appears no higher in the quantitative table because its images are less conspicuous for their number than for their prolongation. The prison scene, the garden scene and the abdication scene best illustrate a type of extended metaphor which appears in great profusion throughout the tragedy. The length of each play must also be kept in mind. Thus *Richard Third* is on the average less figurative than the table indicates, while the reverse holds true for *Macbeth*. The large number of images in the great tragedies and the greater number in *Hamlet, Antony and Cleopatra* and *Macbeth* than in *King Lear, Othello* and *Julius Caesar,* are perhaps worthy of notice.

The second table, arranging the plays in four chronological groups of nine each, shows a rapid increase in the proportion of imaginatively powerful metaphor. The fourth group averages more than half again as many seemingly powerful metaphors as the third, more than twice as many as the second, and more than three and a half times the number in the first. The average increase in the total number of figures recorded is steady but less decisive.

The third table contrasts the dramatic types. Tragedy uses as a rule a more profuse metaphor than comedy. In both comedy and tragedy the more emotional passages are apt to be highly figurative, but a persistently figurative style as a rule elevates the intermediate matter in tragedy. The formalities of metaphor are most apparent in Shakespere in the Histories, with their long and decorous scenes of counsel and debate. The Histories show approximately nine tenths as many figures as the Tragedies, and two and a half times as many as the Comedies. Nevertheless the Comedies average approximately two thirds as many images of high imaginative value as the Histories, and the Tragedies only a little less than twice as many as the Histories. By referring to the dates of the plays it will be seen that the reduction in the number of superficial images from the Histories to the Comedies and from the Comedies to the Tragedies is partly a chronological one. The four Dramatic Romances, *Pericles, Cymbeline, The Winter's Tale* and *The Tempest*, although less richly figurative than the Tragedies, show a greater proportion of stimulating figures than any of the preceding groups. The general tendency of the plays is to become more metaphorical, but even more marked than this is the growing tendency to make imagery tell more definitely on the imagination. In *The Winter's Tale* and *The Tempest* Shakespere seems to husband his metaphor most effectively.

In Table One it may be observed that *The Merry Wives of Windsor* ranks thirty-second among thirty-six plays.

In Table Four this play ranks third. The contrast is readily explained. The dialogue in this comedy is on a relatively low emotional level. Neither the formal language of military parley nor the Euphuistic conceits of shepherdesses and courtiers raise the quantity of metaphor. On the other hand what images there are are for the most part either Falstaff's own or those which the presence of the merry knight is alone sufficient to evoke. In The First Part of *Henry Fourth* Falstaff's humor is highly figurative. The close of the great tavern scene in that play is a banquet of imagery. In the Second Part Falstaff's language may be said, with the recruiting scene and the soliloquy on Shallow well in mind, to be, nevertheless, comparatively restrained in its figures. The tavern scene in the Second Part is more realistic than in the First and comparatively bare of metaphor. Falstaff is quite as clever, perhaps even more clever, but he is more inspired to action than to poetry. In *The Merry Wives* he has for the time being lost much of his self-protective cleverness. He gets little contentment out of the course of events. The only pleasure that remains is to return if possible to the glowing imagination that characterizes his lines in The First Part of *Henry Fourth*. He turns defeat into victory by proving himself less of a fool for his ducking than a wit for describing it metaphorically. The poor fat knight sits by the morning fire with little to reconcile him to life but a glass of sack and a Miltonic imagination.

Metaphor is seldom more sustained at a considerable pitch of poetry than in *Twelfth Night*, never perhaps more gorgeous than in *Antony and Cleopatra*. The imagery of the three Roman plays based on Plutarch deserves a special comment. *Julius Caesar* it will be observed contains an exceptionally large proportion of literal language. *Coriolanus* shows a comparatively large number of figures, but many of these are of a merely formal sort sustaining the unusually consistent dignity of the dialogue. In *Antony and Cleopatra* on the other hand we find the richest, most opulent and most Asiatic imagery in Shakespere. In this tragedy a marked distinction must be made between the Roman and the Egyptian scenes. Augustus and Octavia, like the stoical conspirators in *Julius Caesar,* speak a restrained language. Cleopatra and Antony speak perhaps the most magnificent metaphorical language ever conceived by an English poet. In lavish vegetation of metaphor, Corinthian splendor and golden pomp we read the story of two lovers who offered the world upon the fragrant altar of poetic imagination. Metaphorical animism is a notable feature of Antony's lines, especially during his lapses into moral degradation and despair. He determines the fate of the world by metaphorical logic: "The very dice obey him," he exclaims, as the superior position through the laxity of his policies slips into the hands of Augustus. Here is a far off echo of the metaphorical logic of Richard II. Again in a madness of figurative excess Antony cries of lodging Lichas on the horns of the moon. His tragedy may be considered in part a study in the fatality of such imagination. A world of oriental poetry goes down to defeat before a prosaic world of Roman discipline. The play shows Shakespere's dislike of the prosaic cunning of Augustus, and his bitter grief for those vices which made inevitable and just the tragedy of the Egyptians and their lord. *The Tempest* is on the other hand a reconciliation of poetic imagination and moral discipline. The problem is an often recurring one in Shakespere. Richard II and Bolinbroke, Hamlet and Horatio, Antony and Augustus are but three of the contrasts in character which bring the dilemma to the surface. With impartial justice Shakespere shows the deficiencies of both the over-literal and the over-imaginative mind.

Several of the plays and many of the characters invite

special study. The poet shows a conscious interest in the subject of imagery. No better criticism of Hotspur's celebrated apostrophe to Honor is possible than the comment of the discreet Worcester. When want of breath brings the young enthusiast to a pause, Earl Percy calmly remarks,

> He apprehends a world of figures here,
> But not the form of what he should attend.
>
> I, 3, 209

An artistic unity underlies the metaphors in many of the plays. *Richard Second* has in this respect already been reviewed. In *Macbeth*, except for the artful entrance scene before Dunsinane, imagery is prevailingly nocturnal. In *Othello*, except for two black images of Iago, nothing clashes with the glare which metaphor throws over jealousy. Most of the images in *Romeo and Juliet* would sound amiss in *Troilus and Cressida*. *King John* from the standpoint of its figures seems nearest to a medley. *A Midsummer-Night's Dream* from the same viewpoint preserves a most remarkable unity. Generally speaking the imagery in the early plays is violent, bold and startling yet comparatively conventional. As the poet's art develops his figures become more powerful, more original, more comprehensive, subtler, more intellectual and more beautiful. A height of power is reached in the philosophical images of *King Lear*. An extreme of subtlety lies in the imagery *Antony and Cleopatra*. A consummate harmony of discipline and metaphorically inspired imagination is attained in *The Tempest*.

XI

CONCLUSION

With the illustration and analysis of eight types of poetic metaphor behind us we may proceed to a rapid summary and conclusion. The survey of Elizabethan imagery has shown the Decorative image typically represented in Sir Philip Sidney, the Sunken image typically represented in the subdued metaphors of Daniel, the Violent image, or fustian, represented in Thomas Kyd, the Radical image in Donne, the Intensive image in Spenser, the Expansive image in Bacon, the Exuberant image in Marlowe and the figure of wit and humor in Thomas Nash. Shakespere's "infinite variety" has been acknowledged in the preceding chapter.

The Decorative image is one in which the two terms are as incongruent as metaphor will allow, and so constituted and associated that the imaginative values are reduced to a minimum. A Sunken figure is one which powerfully affects the imagination without conveying a definite picture. In Violent metaphor, or fustian, imagination is restricted by sensationalism, which reduces to a minimum the intellectual elements of the figure, by impetuosity, which blurs the relation of the terms, and by a prevailing conventionality, which hinders a close adjustment of the figure to a particular case. In Radical imagery the minor term is itself of little imaginative value, but the metaphorical relation powerful. The Intensive metaphor is one of high imaginative value in which clarity and concentration associate the minor term with pictorial art. The Expansive image is one in which each term opens a wide vista to the imagination, and one in which each term is strongly

modified by the other. The Exuberant image is characterized by the impressionistic relation of two broad and imaginatively valuable terms. Although no precise description of the metaphors of wit and humor is attempted, they
have been observed in relation to the preceding categories.

The Decorative figure is by definition one which plays
on the confines of metaphor, dares its laws and courts defeat. It supplied the toys which beguiled a belated English culture through a half serious and half playful child-
hood. The naïve pedantries of this imagery have long
fallen into disuse and were a mere passing vogue among
courtiers and fashionable men of letters. The chief interest in a study of such imagination is the clear example
which it offers of a fantastic eccentricity and a relatively
harmless affectation. The form is also of interest from the
part which it played in the early writing of those who later
developed the highest powers of metaphorical language.
Love's Labor's Lost and *The Shepherd's Calendar* precede
the great tragedies and *The Fairie Queene*. Yet this imagery served the sixteenth century writers well, as their
age emerged from a fierce, a stolid or a bucolic tradition
into an elaborate culture. Its great popularity is more ex-
plicable when we consider the emotionally subtle and intellectually naïve temper of the times. Behind this literary
affectation one may often trace the lineaments of moral
skepticism and despair, and of a delicate and sincere emotion.

The Violent image like the conceit is far from the language of distinguished thought or feeling. It is however
a democratic and perennial form, in contrast with that
transient and aristocratic mannerism. Because fustian is
a vice which the world must ever guard against, though
doubtless with ill success, and because the Elizabethans
wrote fustian supremely well and developed it to the verge
of poetry, a study of their Violent metaphor is attractive.

The "insolent" images of Kyd are related to those of the modern sensational newspaper story, wherein "Mary Pickford, bursting with sobs, reveals the miseries of her married life." By a perversity of mind the sophisticated reader smiles a protective smile, and proclaims such metaphor insincere. Fustian is rarely insincere. It is prevailingly ingenuous. The man of fustian is powerless as a personal foe but formidable as a demagogue. Antony with the mob behind him defeats Brutus, while Octavius defeats Antony in the strategy of war.

The Radical image is like a sharp knife. In the hands of an unpracticed writer it may well do more harm than good. Yet with such an instrument Donne transforms objects seemingly incapable of imaginative value. Of this figure we may say, be bold, be bold, be not too bold. Truth is its goal. The realist employs it bravely. The mystic uses it humbly, since there is no pretense that its two terms are of equivalent imaginative value. He will not liken Divinity to the might of the ocean, but to the perfection of a circle. The discovery of poetic images in neutral sources is typical of the daring of Elizabethan imagination. The brave catholic idealism of the old dramatists spurned a cloying, saccharine, narrowly aristocratic imagery and sent the breath of poetry over charred wood and frozen loam. The magic of the humblest Elizabethans raised beauty from the dust. The modern poet feels the glow of fellowship with his courageous predecessors in English song.

The Sunken image is subdued in form but powerful and effective. It is acceptable alike to classical and romantic taste, to Corneille and Shakespere, to the criticism of Voltaire and that of Charles Lamb. Especially in reflective poetry such as that of Wordsworth or Samuel Daniel it seems appropriate. It invigorates, elevates and ennobles the language of Shakespere, and makes poignant the lines of Spenser.

A study of Intensive imagery illustrates the kinship between literature and the fine arts. Emblems and personifications are its principal devices. The emblems of heraldry, of religion, and the classical traditions in the secular
ritual of poetry, figures which after two thousand years are
still in the process of perfection at the hands of the guild
of poets, were handled by the Elizabethans with great
delicacy and a right reverence. New flowers were woven
into the imperishable garland of Meleager. Spenser shows
the personification with fineness of feeling, delicacy of
color, beauty, dignity and philosophical worth. The Intensive figure is particularly adapted to the expression of
ideals thoroughly established in the mind of the poet and
his public. It is rather the metaphor of adoration than
that of contemplation. The latter develops a plastic
thought or molds the reader's mind to new conceptions.
The poetry of adoration confers a formal beauty upon the
accepted premises of an ideal life. Through the Intensive
image in poetry, pageantry, religion and ceremony the
Elizabethan age found eloquent expression for its foremost
values. The form suffered a rapid decline after the lifetime of Shakespere. The Puritans turned from the Intensive Imagery of Catholic ritual to the Expansive Imagery
of the Old Testament. Though we are in some respects
more the masters of this metaphor than the old poets, our
mastery is much less widely effective and less spontaneous.

On the subject of allegory no one has spoken better than
Dowden in the following passage. ''But the special virtue
of *The Fairie Queene* will be found only by one who receives it neither as pageantry nor as philosophy, but in the
way in which Spenser meant it should be received—as a
living creature of the imagination, a spirit incarnate, 'one
altogether' 'of reasonable soul and human flesh subsist-
ing.' ''—If Dowden is correct in his example, no writer has
as yet attempted a synthetic criticism of *The Fairie Queene*.

Expansive imagery is equally the language of emotion and of contemplation. The earlier tragedy adapted this metaphor in a somewhat naïve but impressive philosophy, while the philosophy of Bacon is buttressed by figures almost as magnificent as those of his chief dramatic contemporaries. Beauty, terror and the sense of power expand the imagination. Above all in the metaphors of reflection we see the marvelous rapidity and comprehension and the revealing function of metaphorical thought. The magic of the poets is nowhere more in evidence than in those figures which make of the sum of familiar experiences an image that carries us afar into the ways of poetry. Thus among opulent metaphor in the death-scene of Shakespere's Antony we find expressions of the utmost simplicity:

> the long day's task is done,
> And we must sleep.

In Exuberant imagery terms are in an elemental relation. The more rational distinctions of sophisticated art are often cast aside and two ideas related only, for example, by a common splendor. Exuberant also are the magnificent hyperboles of Marlowe, and those elusive images in which the arts of two or more senses are fused in vague metaphorical relations. Strong religious experiences record many such expressions. The metaphors arising from music though as yet indistinct promise to become a new glory to poetic thought. Images that look rather backward than forward are those recurrences of pagan animism in modern poetry which leave the romanticist in a rapture and the classicist cold. At least since the days when Richard of Bury wrote his *Philobiblon* Englishmen have shown an unusual fondness for exuberant metaphor.

The images of wit and humor in Elizabethan literature are less keen, less whetted and less ironically bitter and subtle than figures to be found in later periods of our

literary history. But for gothic extravagances of drawing, for Rabelaisian humor with not infrequently a genuine
appeal to the intellect beneath its uncouth forms, and for
the metaphors of delicate fancy, plain mirth and English
fun, no age exceeds that of Elizabeth's England. Elizabethan poets found in the metaphorical mind on the one
hand a stimulus to intensity of thought and feeling, on the
other a relaxation in the delicate or the grotesque. The
comic spirit took upon itself in the Age of Shakespere less
responsibility than to-day, but improved to the uttermost
life's gaity and mirth. How far this philosophy was
superficial and how far wise who is wise enough to say?
It is not an imaginary clown but an age that sings the song
in *As You Like It:*

> This carol they began that hour,
>   With a hey, and a ho, and a hey nonino,
> How that a life is but a flower
>   In the spring time.

The last word concerning Elizabethan imagery, which is
so largely rationalistic, should be a recognition of its power
to embody ideals. The psychology which made this power
possible is veiled but not damaged in the modern world of
business and industry. A study of Elizabethan metaphors
teaches us a catholicity in the choice of objects and an
equally intimate touch between imagistic poetry and the
ideals of living. The beauty of the Elizabethan images is
prevailingly of the world of men, and their language is
powerful to all mankind. They challenge the poets and
artists of our own day to embody their own ideals, to search
the achievements of mechanics, the newly discovered micro-
cosm of cells within the body, the worlds of the physicist
and the astronomer, and, with a fuller knowledge of our
life-forces, to raise new standards to which men may lift
their eyes and from which new inspiration may be caught.

Elizabethan imagery represents a power gained but not consolidated by the Anglo-Saxon mind. The writers of the closet drama of the nineteenth century attempted an antiquarian reproduction. They clung too much to the letter of the past and felt too little the resilience of history. In Elizabethan imagery there is something to discard, little to imitate and much to admire.